SOCIAL and EMOTIONAL LEARNING

Education at SAGE

SAGE is a leading international publisher of journals, books, and electronic media for academic, educational, and professional markets.

Our education publishing includes:

- accessible and comprehensive texts for aspiring education professionals and practitioners looking to further their careers through continuing professional development

- inspirational advice and guidance for the classroom

- authoritative state of the art reference from the leading authors in the field

Find out more at: **www.sagepub.co.uk/education**

SOCIAL and EMOTIONAL LEARNING

a critical appraisal

NEIL HUMPHREY

Los Angeles | London | New Delhi
Singapore | Washington DC

Los Angeles | London | New Delhi
Singapore | Washington DC

SAGE Publications Ltd
1 Oliver's Yard
55 City Road
London EC1Y 1SP

SAGE Publications Inc.
2455 Teller Road
Thousand Oaks, California 91320

SAGE Publications India Pvt Ltd
B 1/I 1 Mohan Cooperative Industrial Area
Mathura Road
New Delhi 110 044

SAGE Publications Asia-Pacific Pte Ltd
3 Church Street
#10-04 Samsung Hub
Singapore 049483

© Neil Humphrey, 2013

First published 2013

Library of Congress Control Number: 2012947267

British Library Cataloguing in Publication data

A catalogue record for this book is available from the British Library

Editor: Marianne Lagrange
Editorial assistant: Kathryn Bromwich
Project manager: Bill Antrobus
Production editor: Thea Watson
Copyeditor: Peter Williams
Proofreader: Caroline Stock
Marketing manager: Catherine Slinn
Cover design: Naomi Robinson
Typeset by Kestrel Data, Exeter, Devon
Printed in Great Britain by:
CPI Group (UK) Ltd, Croydon, CR0 4YY

ISBN 978-1-4462-5695-4
ISBN 978-1-4462-5696-1 (pbk)

MIX
Paper from
responsible sources
FSC
www.fsc.org   FSC® C013604

For Angela and Beth

Contents

List of abbreviations

ABCD	Affective-Behavioural-Cognitive-Dynamic
ACER	Australian Council for Educational Research
ACES	Assessment of Children's Emotional Skills
AGDHA	Australian Government Department of Health and Ageing
CASEL	Collaborative for Academic, Social and Emotional Learning
CDCP	Centers for Disease Control and Prevention
CDP	Child Development Project
CfC	Committee for Children
CMHS	Center for Mental Health Services
CSC	Caring School Community
CSVP	Centre for the Study of Violence Prevention
DENI	Department for Education in Northern Ireland
EDS	Emotional Dysregulation Scale
EI	emotional intelligence
ELAI	Emotional Literacy Assessment Instrument
EQi-YV	Emotional Quotient Inventory – Youth Version
HOCESC	House of Commons Education and Skills Committee
IES	Institute of Education Sciences
IGPA	Institute of Government and Public Affairs
IPPR	Institute for Public Policy Research
IQ	implementation quality
LA	local authority
LLW	Learning for Life and Work
MESSY	Matson Evaluation of Social Skills in Youngsters
MSCEIT-YV	Mayer-Salovey-Caruso Emotional Intelligence Test – Youth Version

NAE	National Agency for Education
NCLB	No Child Left Behind Act 2001 (US)
NICE	National Institute for Health and Clinical Excellence
NRCIM	National Research Council and Institute of Medicine
PATHS	Promoting Alternative Thinking Strategies
PDMU	Personal Development and Mutual Understanding
PEHW	Pupils' Emotional Health and Wellbeing
RCT	randomised controlled trial
REDI	Research-Based Developmentally Informed
SACDRC	Social and Character Development Research Consortium
SAFE	Sequenced, Active, Focused, Explicit
SAT	standard assessment task/test
SCCP	School as a Caring Community Profile
SEAL	Social and Emotional Aspects of Learning
SEARS	Social-Emotional Assets and Resilience Scales
SECD	social, emotional and character development
SEEAE	social, emotional, ethical and academic education
SEL	social and emotional learning
SET	Social and Emotional Training
SSIS	Social Skills Improvement System
SSRS	Social Skills Rating System
TaMHS	Targeted Mental Health in Schools
TEIQue	Trait Emotional Intelligence Questionnaire
UNICEF	United Nations Children's Emergency Fund
USDHHS	US Department of Health and Human Services

Acknowledgements

I am deeply grateful to Drs Ann Lendrum and Michael Wigelsworth for their support, advice and encouragement during the writing of this book.

About the author

Neil Humphrey is Professor of Psychology of Education at the University of Manchester. Social and emotional learning is his central research interest. Neil has led (or collaborated on) a number of high-profile studies in this area, including the national evaluations of the primary social and emotional aspects of learning (SEAL) small-group work element, secondary SEAL programme and the Targeted Mental Health in Schools (TaMHS) initiative. His most recent project is a major randomised controlled trial of the Promoting Alternative Thinking Strategies (PATHS) curriculum. Neil has published extensively on social and emotional learning in journals such as *Educational Psychology, School Mental Health, Educational and Psychological Measurement* and *Child and Adolescent Mental Health*.

1

Introduction

Overview

The aim of this chapter is to provide the reader with a broad overview of the field of social and emotional learning (SEL) and a rationale for this book. In doing so I touch upon some of the key issues that are addressed in more depth later in the text. The chapter concludes with a brief look at the structure and content of the book in order to give the reader a sense of what is to follow.

Key Points

- SEL is a dominant orthodoxy in education systems across the world.
- It refers to the process of explicitly developing skills such as empathy and self-regulation in children and adults, typically in school settings.
- SEL interventions vary in their reach, component structure and prescriptiveness.
- Research on the implementation and outcomes of SEL programmes has yielded promising results, but there are a number of problematic issues with the current evidence base.

Rationale for the text

SEL is currently the zeitgeist in education. It has captured the imagination of academics, policy-makers and practitioners alike in recent years. To many, SEL is the 'missing piece' in the quest to provide effective education for all children and young people (Elias, 1997). They claim that school-based promotion of SEL will lead to a range of positive outcomes for children and young people, including increased social and emotional competence, improvements in academic attainment, better behaviour and reduced mental health problems (Durlak et al., 2011). To others, the increased interest in SEL represents the latest in a series of classroom fads (Paul and Elder, 2007), or a worrying example of the 'therapeutic turn' taken recently in education and society more generally (Furedi, 2003, 2009). They argue that SEL is, at best, a waste of time and resources (Craig, 2007). At worst, it is seen as a corrosive influence that distracts schools from their primary purpose of educating children and young people (Ecclestone and Hayes, 2008).

 Points for Reflection

- What is your view on the role of SEL in education?

The aim of this book is to provide a critical appraisal of the field. What I hope will set it apart from the many other books available on this topic is, firstly, that it will take a balanced, analytical approach throughout. I do not intend to promote SEL as a panacea for all that ails education. Nor do I wish to endorse the argument that it is a potentially damaging influence on children and young people. It is up to you, as the reader, to make up your own mind. I will simply present the evidence as I see it, which brings us to the second distinguishing characteristic of the book: a clear focus on research. The ideas and arguments presented throughout *Social and Emotional Learning: A Critical Appraisal* are grounded in research findings, drawn from around the world. A truly international scope is – I hope – the third 'unique selling point'. SEL is a global phenomenon and this is reflected throughout the book. Finally, the analysis presented in these pages benefits from the inclusion of the very latest developments in the field, including a seminal meta-analysis of empirical findings relating to the impact of school-based SEL interventions (Durlak et al., 2011).

What is SEL?

In this brief introductory chapter I hope to highlight some of the key issues that will be addressed in the book. So, where do we begin? A working definition of SEL would certainly be helpful. As we will see in Chapter 2, there is a significant degree of ambiguity and conceptual confusion evident in attempts to set parameters on what is (and is not) SEL (Hoffman, 2009). In the meantime, consider the following widely used definition provided by the Collaborative for Academic, Social and Emotional Learning (CASEL). CASEL define SEL as:

> a process for helping children and even adults develop the fundamental skills for life effectiveness. SEL teaches the skills we all need to handle ourselves, our relationships and our work effectively and ethically. These skills include recognising and managing our emotions, developing caring and concern for others, establishing positive relationships, making responsible decisions, and handling challenging situations constructively and ethically. They are the skills that allow children to calm themselves when angry, make friends, resolve conflicts respectfully, and make ethical and safe choices. (http://www.casel.org)

 Points for Reflection

- How does this definition of SEL fit with your own?
- What assumptions and values are embedded in the prevailing view of SEL?

Let's briefly break this definition down. Firstly, SEL is a *process*. It's a course of action, a method or practice in which schools engage. Secondly, SEL is for *children and adults*, each and every member of the school community. Thirdly, SEL teaches skills that *we all need* and are *fundamental for life effectiveness*. Thus it is a universal, essential process. Fourthly, the skills endowed through SEL are *social-emotional* in nature, relating to both *intrapersonal* (within the individual – such as being able to manage one's emotions) and *interpersonal* (between the individual and others – such as establishing positive relationships) domains. The key components of this definition and its assumptions and implications have been critiqued from a variety of perspectives (e.g. Ecclestone and Hayes, 2009; Hoffman, 2009; Watson et al., 2012), but this is something we will address later. For now, it at least gives us a broad idea of what we mean when we talk about *social and emotional learning*.

SEL has become increasingly important in educational research, policy and practice in recent years. Indeed, it is not unreasonable to suggest that it has perhaps become *the* dominant orthodoxy in education worldwide. As evidence of this, consider that in the United States (US), a landmark bill was recently introduced to the House of Representatives that changed federal education policy to promote SEL (including, for example, amendments to existing legislation in order to enable funding for teacher training and continuing professional development to be used for SEL programming) (Biggert et al., 2011). Furthermore, in most US states, SEL is integrated into mandated K-12 learning standards, with one state (Illinois) having explicit, free-standing SEL goals and benchmarks (Dusenbury et al., 2011). Educators attempt to meet these standards by implementing one (or more) of a plethora of programmes. There were in excess of 240 of these programmes available a decade ago (CASEL, 2003), a number which is only likely to have increased since then.

A similar picture has emerged in other countries. In England, for example, our last government introduced a range of policy initiatives that either directly or indirectly addressed SEL. The most well-known of these was the social and emotional aspects of learning (SEAL) programme (Department for Children, Schools and Families, 2007; Department for Education and Skills, 2005a), a national strategy which was estimated to be in use in 90 per cent of primary and 70 per cent of secondary schools by 2010 (Humphrey et al., 2010). In Australia, the KidsMatter (early childhood and primary school) and MindMatters (secondary school) SEL initiatives have been rolled out to every state and territory (Ainley et al., 2006; Slee et al., 2009). Education systems in many other nations – including Spain, Portugal, Finland, Singapore, Canada, Sweden and Germany – have also embraced SEL (Marcelino Botín Foundation, 2011).

A taxonomy of SEL

SEL programmes take a variety of forms. To begin to make sense of what can, at first, seem like a bewildering array, it may be useful to consider the following fundamental intervention characteristics. This taxonomy is derived from key reviews and texts in the field (e.g. Durlak et al., 2011; Weare and Nind, 2011; Wilson and Lipsey, 2007). The three dimensions are presented briefly below before each is discussed in more detail.

Firstly, it is possible to distinguish between:

- *universal* interventions, developed with the intention of delivery to the entire student body;

- *targeted/indicated* interventions, designed to provide focused input for students at risk of (or already experiencing) social, emotional and behavioural difficulties.

It is worth noting that, from the outset, although I make reference to targeted/indicated approaches at certain points, the primary focus of this book is on universal SEL interventions. This is because these approaches are much more closely aligned with the underlying theory, philosophy, assumptions and values of the field (see Chapter 2).

We can also consider the extent to which an intervention pervades different aspects of school life. Typically, distinctions are made between:

- interventions that emphasise the delivery of a taught *curriculum*;

- those designed to change aspects of the *school environment or ethos*;

- programmes that involve work with *parents and/or the wider community*;

- those that involve some *combination* of these components.

Finally, we might also consider the level of prescriptiveness inherent in the programme guidance. Here, a distinction is usually made between:

- interventions that are *top-down* in nature, providing detailed, structured guidance on implementation procedures, with an implicit assumption that they will be carried out faithfully;

- programmes that are *bottom-up* in nature, emphasising flexibility and local adaptation in implementation.

Dimension 1: intervention reach

Perhaps the most basic distinction that can be made in the SEL literature is between programmes that are designed for delivery to the entire student body ('universal' interventions) and those that provide focused intervention for those children at risk of or already experiencing social, emotional and behavioural difficulties ('targeted/indicated' interventions). Beyond the fundamental difference of their reach, universal and targeted/indicated interventions also differ in a number of other important ways:

- Universal SEL interventions reflect a preventive approach, where the emphasis is on equipping children and young people with the skills they need to become resilient to the onset of difficulties. Targeted/indicated interventions are, by definition, reactive in nature, and therefore concerned with remediating existing problems.

- Given their nature and the fact they are often delivered in withdrawal sessions, targeted/indicated interventions can be associated with stigma for participating children; universal interventions are generally considered to be more 'inclusive' since every child takes part and there is less focus on within-child problems (Reicher, 2010).

- Universal SEL interventions tend to be fairly 'light touch' in nature, but are typically delivered over a prolonged time period (often throughout the school year); by contrast, targeted/indicated interventions are more intensive, reflecting the greater needs of the children involved.

- Research demonstrates greater change in outcomes for children participating in targeted/indicated interventions than for those involved in universal programmes (Wilson and Lipsey, 2007). However, this reflects the fact that there is greater 'room for improvement' in key outcome variables among children selected for targeted interventions.

A balance between universal and targeted provision in schools is typically recommended. Indeed, some of the more recently developed programmes incorporate both. Examples include the KidsMatter initiative in Australia (Commonwealth of Australia, 2009) and the SEAL programme in England (Department for Education and Skills, 2006, 2007a). However, research tells us that many schools still work primarily from a 'reactive' model. For instance, in a recent scoping survey of school-based provision in England, 71 per cent of schools reported that their central focus was on helping children with existing or developing problems (Vostanis et al., 2012).

Dimension 2: component structure

The second dimension in our SEL taxonomy is the structural composition of the intervention itself. Here we can distinguish between programmes that comprise primarily a single component and those that involve multiple components. Although there is no complete consensus, reviews of research (e.g. Adi et al., 2007; Blank et al., 2009) typically identify three common components:

- *A taught curriculum* – typically taking the form of a series of teacher-led lessons and activities designed to help children develop the social and emotional skills outlined earlier in this chapter.

- *School environment* – although somewhat more protean than other components, this would usually include activity in a range of areas (for example, revisions to school policies and rules) focused on improving the school's ethos/climate, so that as an institution it more closely embodies the values embedded in SEL.

- *Parents and the wider community* – programmes including this component incorporate a particular focus on broadening the reach of SEL beyond the immediate school environment. This could include parenting support, community projects and so on.

There are two important qualifying statements relating to this dimension. The first is to note that its utility in classifying SEL programmes is at the broadest level only. For example, even the archetypal curricular interventions typically contain at least some element of the other two (e.g. homework activities to be completed with parents to enable consolidation and generalisation of skills). The second issue to note is that there is by no means an equal balance between programmes that focus mainly on one or some combination of these factors. For example, Blank et al.'s (2009) review of universal SEL approaches in secondary education found that the overwhelming majority were primarily curriculum-based, with only a handful incorporating the other two components. Similarly, Durlak et al.'s (2011) meta-analysis reported that multi-component programmes comprised only a quarter of the evidence base.

Dimension 3: prescriptiveness

The level of prescriptiveness inherent in a given programme is an issue that has received scant attention until recently. This is due in part to the historical dominance of highly prescriptive approaches to SEL. It is only in the last few years that more flexible programmes have started to emerge. Another contributory factor is the increased attention that has been paid to implementation in recent years – in particular the fidelity-adaptation debate (see Chapter 5).

Prescriptive SEL programmes (such as the Second Step programme in the US) are usually curriculum-based and typically provide very detailed manuals that instruct school staff in the appropriate manner of delivery in a step-by-step fashion. There is a single, preferred model of implementation and lessons are often provided in the form of a comprehensive script. This is expected to lead to better quality implementation, because manualisation can provide a scaffold for school staff, giving them structure and organisation, a clear plan of what do to and guidance on how they should do it (Gottfredson and Gottfredson, 2002).

By contrast, flexible approaches to SEL (such as the secondary SEAL programme in England) emphasise choice, local ownership and goodness of fit with local context. School staff may therefore be encouraged to choose the specific aspects of a programme that they wish to deliver, in addition to developing their own materials and/or supplementing with other activities. Sitting somewhere in the middle are approaches that offer both a degree of flexibility and an inherent structure, but at different levels (such as the KidsMatter programme in Australia).

The above taxonomy provides a useful starting point for our understanding of the nature of SEL programmes. However, it is important to note that there are several other ways in which they may differ. For example, what is the modality of the intervention? Programmes may use behavioural strategies, cognitively-oriented approaches, social skills training, and so on. I have opted not to include this aspect in the main taxonomy because these modalities are not mutually exclusive. Also, most SEL programmes reflect a blend rather than a single orientation. Finally, where analysis has been undertaken, the evidence suggests they produce largely similar effects (Wilson and Lipsey, 2007).

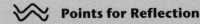

Points for Reflection

- How does the composition of an SEL programme reflect underlying assumptions and values of programme developers?

Why has SEL become so popular?

Why has there been such interest and enthusiasm for SEL across the world? The reasons are manifold and will be explored in more detail in Chapter 3, but three commonly cited benefits of SEL are central:

- *Preventive* utility, whereby SEL helps to 'inoculate' children and young people from a variety of negative outcomes, such as emotional and behavioural difficulties.

- SEL *promotes* a range of desirable outcomes, such as increased social competence.

- These two properties make children more effective learners, thus *increasing academic attainment.*

The third benefit noted above is particularly crucial given the increasing emphasis on academic standards and test scores in education systems around the world. However, as we will see in Chapter 7, it is also a somewhat controversial claim.

Bringing these ideas together, the guidance for schools in the secondary version of the aforementioned SEAL programme in England told teachers that they could expect

> better academic results for all pupils and schools; more effective learning . . . higher motivation; better behaviour; higher school attendance; more responsible pupils, who are better citizens and more able to contribute to society; lower levels of stress and anxiety; higher morale, performance and retention of staff; [and] a more positive school ethos. (Department for Children, Schools and Families, 2007: 8–9)

Given such claims, it is not difficult to understand why such programmes have been so beguiling to educators.

However, the view of SEL as a universal remedy is complicated by several factors. SEL programmes are extremely heterogeneous. They vary greatly in their nature, audience, settings and expected outcomes. This makes prescriptive claims about their benefits rather problematic, especially given the variety and different forms they may take. It is fair to say that no single SEL programme has been proven to improve all (or even most) of the outcomes listed above. This does not stop the claims made creating a level of expectation among school staff that cannot realistically be met, and which may subsequently act as a barrier to sustained implementation efforts. For example, consider the aforementioned SEAL programme. In our recent national evaluation (Humphrey et al., 2010), we found that expectations of what secondary SEAL could achieve varied wildly within and between schools. There was no 'common vision', and staff often had extremely grandiose ideas about the amount of improvement in outcomes that the programme would bring about. When these expectations were not met in the early years of the programme, many staff began to withdraw their efforts.

What can research tell us about SEL?

The issues noted above have been addressed in part by attempts to delineate the different SEL programmes and provide assessments of their evidential bases. For example, we might look to:

- *Safe and Sound: An Educational Leader's Guide to Evidence-Based Social and Emotional Learning Programs* (CASEL, 2003). This text describes and rates 80 programmes in relation to the outcomes they target and the evidence for their effectiveness.

- The *National Registry of Evidence-Based Programs and Practices* (http://nrepp.samhsa.gov/). The Registry provides a searchable directory of interventions that encompass SEL programmes under the broader umbrella of 'mental health promotion'.

- The *Blueprints for Violence Prevention* database (http://www. colorado.edu/cspv/blueprints/matrix.html). The database helpfully distinguishes between *model* and *promising* programmes. This distinction is based upon independent judgements of the quality of evaluation research, sustained effects and multiple site replications.

Brief examination of such resources quickly separates the 'wheat from the chaff'. The Blueprints project, for example, recommends only 11 interventions from over 900 as meeting their 'model program' criteria, and 20 as meeting their 'promising program' criteria. Of these, some (such as the Incredible Years and Promoting Alternative Thinking Strategies curricula) are what we might call 'bona fide' SEL approaches (in that their central aims, content and outcomes are social-emotional in nature). While this demonstrates that there are several 'proven' SEL interventions, it also highlights the fact that the evidence base for the majority is still developing.

A recent meta-analysis of universal school-based SEL programmes by CASEL (Durlak et al., 2011) highlights further issues with the evidence base. This paper represents the most up-to-date and comprehensive analysis of the evidence for SEL, with 213 studies included, representing outcomes for nearly a quarter of a million children and young people. The authors reported very promising findings, with children involved in SEL interventions demonstrating improved social and emotional skills, academic attainment, attitudes and behaviour, when compared to controls (e.g. those not involved in SEL interventions). However, they also reported a high level of variability in the quality of studies:

- 53 per cent relied solely on child self-report, raising issues of reliability in studies involving younger children;

- 42 per cent did not monitor implementation in any way, meaning what school staff actually did and, in particular, how closely they stuck to intervention guidelines was unknown;

- 19 per cent were unpublished reports and therefore not subjected to academic scrutiny;

- 24 per cent used measures with no reported reliability, meaning that they may not tap consistent responses over time;

- 49 per cent used measures with no reported validity, meaning that they may not measure what they purport to measure.

So, although the evidence fairly consistently points towards the positive outcomes of SEL interventions, we know that there are quality issues inherent in the research literature. This suggests that a degree of caution may be required in interpreting the outcomes of studies.

Why is research – and in particular, the quality of research – such an important consideration in the analysis presented in this book?

Put simply, SEL interventions incur significant investment of time and resources (human, financial, material) on the part of participating schools. Now more than ever (given the current fiscal and educational climates), schools need reassurance that such an undertaking is worth their while. They need to know if there is strong evidence that a given intervention is likely to produce a set of desired outcomes. Keeping research evidence central to the decision-making process for schools interested in implementing SEL interventions helps to guard against the 'crass, profit-driven, and socially and scientifically irresponsible' (Sternberg, 2002: xii) side of the 'industry'. As a case in point, consider the case of the School of Emotional Literacy, a UK-based SEL organisation. During the major upsurge in interest in SEL in the UK in the last decade, various local authorities (LAs) spent a total of £300,000 sending teachers on emotional literacy courses provided by the School of Emotional Literacy, until it was revealed that the courses were not accredited (as had been advertised) and were delivered by a trainer whose professional qualifications were spurious (including a doctorate from an Internet-based 'university' in Vanuatu, a tiny island in the South Pacific) (Milne, 2008).

Research (and the kinds of research-based databases noted above) can therefore help to distinguish between the proven SEL programmes, those whose evidence base is still developing and those that may be nothing more than snake oil. As Merrell and Gueldner (2010) state, 'It is usually as waste of time and resources – and is potentially risky – to implement a program that has no or shaky evidence that it will produce the desired results' (p. 29). However, even with those interventions for which there exists a robust evidence base, the journey from research to practice can be complicated (Durlak and DuPre, 2008). Of particular note here is the difference between the environments of highly controlled, well-supported research studies ('efficacy' trials) and the complex, messy world of everyday school practice. The SEL evidence base is primarily composed of research in the former at the expense of the latter. The potential dangers of such disparity were highlighted by Shucksmith and colleagues (2007):

> Studies . . . have seen the investment of massive sums of money in large multi-component longitudinal trials. The results that emerge from these are very useful and are showing the way towards the design of more effective interventions, yet there must be serious doubts as to the availability of such resources within normal education budgets. (p. 5)

These concerns, echoed by Greenberg et al. (2005), are well founded. Where research is conducted on SEL interventions in typical practice conditions ('effectiveness' trials) schools often fail to replicate reported intervention effects (e.g. Kam et al., 2003).

> ∿ **Points for Reflection**
>
> • How important is research evidence compared to what 'feels right'?

The importance of implementation

The problems experienced in bringing evidence-based SEL programmes 'to scale' (e.g. Elias et al., 2003) in normal school settings reinforces the need to explore an area that has only recently begun to attract the attention it deserves: *implementation*. If research on outcomes answers the 'what' in SEL evaluation, implementation research answers the 'how' and 'why'. Thus implementation studies consider aspects of programme delivery such as:

- dosage (e.g. how many sessions were delivered?)

- fidelity (e.g. how closely did the teacher stick to the intervention manual?)

- reach (e.g. was the intervention delivered throughout the school?)

Such studies are also concerned with the factors that influence these (e.g. staff attitudes, time and resources, support from school leadership) (Durlak and DuPre, 2008). The findings of such research have yielded fascinating insights into the processes that underpin the promotion of the range of outcomes highlighted above. First and foremost, *implementation matters*. Reviews of the literature (e.g. Durlak and DuPre, 2008; Greenberg et al., 2005) have shown that the different aspects of implementation can each influence the outcomes of a given intervention. This helps to explain why SEL programmes may be less successful when they are rolled out in real-world settings, where they essentially become diluted among competing pressures and with less support available. However, that is not to say that positive outcomes can only be achieved when school staff stick rigidly to the programme 'script'. Indeed, expecting them to do so is unrealistic. They are professional educators working in unique contexts and circumstances, and as such some degree of adaptation is inevitable. In light of this, one important finding from a major review of over 500 studies conducted by Durlak and DuPre (2008) was that positive results could be achieved with around 60–80 per cent implementation fidelity. This has led to discussion of how to promote the correct balance between fidelity to programme manuals and procedures on the one hand, and adaptation to local needs and circumstances on the other. The implications of these issues will be examined in more detail in Chapter 6.

The structure of this book

Although we have only touched upon a selection of the fundamental issues that will be explored in the ensuing chapters, I hope that this brief introduction has convinced you of the need for a critical appraisal of the field of SEL. In the closing section of this chapter, I provide a concise overview of the structure and content of the book. In planning the organisation of the text, I have attempted to provide comprehensive coverage of the fundamental issues relating to SEL, and to present them in a sequence that makes sense from the point of view of creating a coherent narrative.

In Chapter 2, I provide a critical analysis of the conceptualisation of SEL in the academic and practitioner literature. It uses the aforementioned CASEL definition as a starting point, before exploring alternative conceptualisations and related terms such as 'emotional intelligence'. An examination of the general discourse around SEL is presented, and the implications for theory, research and practice of the inherently protean nature of the concept are discussed. The chapter then outlines and appraises SEL theory – that is, the underlying logic model that connects school-based promotion of SEL to a range of positive outcomes.

Chapter 3 considers how SEL came to be a dominant orthodoxy in education. The influences on the development of the field, including the various conceptualisations of social, emotional and multiple intelligences, progressive education, the concept of resilience, the field of prevention and the self-esteem movement are outlined and discussed. The chapter concludes by considering the political and economic drivers of SEL.

Chapter 4 comprises an international analysis of the current state of SEL in education. Exemplar case studies are provided, including the USA, England, Australia, Sweden and elsewhere. Each case study explores the influence of SEL at both policy and practice levels. The US case study, for example, examines the various state-level SEL standards and recent national legislation (e.g. the Academic, Social and Emotional Learning Act 2011), in addition to a sampling of the proliferation of school-based programmes, such as Promoting Alternative Thinking Strategies (PATHS) and the Caring School Community (Child Development Project). I then explore how cultural differences have influenced the shape SEL has taken in different countries. In particular, I discuss the top-down (primarily the USA) versus bottom-up (primarily Europe and Australia) schism in the design and implementation of approaches to SEL.

Chapter 5 examines the processes involved in the assessment and monitoring of SEL, addressing core questions such as what should be evaluated (e.g. proximal vs. distal outcome variables, assessment of process) and whose perspective should be prioritised. There is a particular focus on the assessment of children's social and emotional competence, with discussion of key issues including the underlying theory and frameworks, the scope and distinctiveness of measures, approaches to assessment (e.g. observation, sociometric techniques, questionnaires), the assessment of maximal (ability) versus typical (trait) behaviour, implementation characteristics and psychometric properties of measures. A range of exemplar measures are reviewed.

In Chapter 6, the focus of the book shifts to how schools implement approaches to SEL and the impact this has on outcomes. Drawing upon seminal work (e.g. Durlak and DuPre, 2008), I outline and discuss the different components of implementation (e.g. fidelity, dosage, quality) and the contextual factors that have been shown to influence them (e.g. implementer characteristics, organisational capacity, programme characteristics). A key area of focus in the implementation literature – the balance between fidelity and adaptation – is examined in detail.

Chapter 7 examines the impact of approaches to SEL on a variety of outcomes, including social and emotional competence, attitudes, pro-social behaviour, mental health and academic achievement. I provide a critical review of research in the field, discussing issues relating to cost-effectiveness, the role of programme developers in evaluations, confirmation bias and adverse effects, and the basic question of what constitutes a good outcome. The chapter concludes by considering examples of outcome research whose findings have 'gone against the grain' (e.g. Humphrey et al., 2010; Social and Character Development Research Consortium, 2010) and analysing them through the lens of Raudenbush's (2008) model for the interpretation of null results.

In concluding the book, Chapter 8 draws together and summarises the key themes developed throughout the preceding chapters. I build upon these to make a series of recommendations for future research, including the need for a new wave of effectiveness studies, an increase in high-quality research beyond the United States, a broadening of focus in implementation evaluation, and detailed modelling of the cost-benefits and cost-effectiveness of SEL.

Notes on voice, terminology and textual features

I write primarily in the first person singular ('I') and plural ('we') throughout the book. This is to impart a more inclusive tone and make the text less impersonal (I am used to writing in academic journals where you are typically required to refer to yourself as 'the current author'!).

It is also worth pointing out from the outset that I refer to 'programmes', 'interventions', 'approaches', etc., interchangeably throughout the book. This is done in the interest of variety, and in the absence of any evidence that they actually describe different things when used in reference to SEL.

At the beginning of each chapter I present key points that summarise the content that follows. Think of this as the 'bite-size' version of the chapter for the reader in a hurry!

As you will have already seen, the text is interspersed with 'points for reflection'. These are included at key points to encourage you as the reader to consider critical issues raised in the text from your own point of view. You are by no means bound to agree with the arguments I put forward!

Finally, at the end of each chapter I make some recommendations for further reading. There is an emphasis on key texts by expert authors that link to and extend the chapter content.

Further Reading

Ecclestone, K. and Hayes, D. (2008) *The Dangerous Rise of Therapeutic Education.* London: Routledge.

Merrell, K. and Gueldner, B. A. (2010). *Social and Emotional Learning in the Classroom: Promoting Mental Health and Academic Success.* London: Guilford Press.

2

What do we mean by social and emotional learning?

Overview

The aim of this chapter is to critically examine the concept of SEL. This begins with an analysis of the prevailing definition in the field, and continues by considering the broader discourse, including related terms such as 'emotional intelligence' and 'well-being'. The chapter concludes with an exploration of the logic model of SEL.

Key Points

- Key components of the prevailing definition of SEL include: (a) that it is a process through which social and emotional skills are explicitly taught; (b) that this process be applied universally (e.g. that this is something we all need); and (c) that developmental psychological theory provides a framework to aid our understanding of which skills are important.
- This definition of SEL also carries with it a number of problematic assumptions and values, including a failure to account for cultural variation in emotional experience and expression.
- There is a distinct lack of clarity in the broader discourse surrounding SEL.
- The logic model provides a plausible account of the processes by which SEL interventions may improve key outcomes for children and young people, but there are gaps and inconsistencies in the evidence base.

It may at first seem rather unnecessary to devote an entire chapter of this book to the task of defining SEL. However, what is (and is not) SEL is by no means set in stone. Developing a clear definition is also a fundamental scientific requirement. Furthermore, where the parameters of SEL are set has important implications for how we view the evidence base in this area. For example, it helps us to decide which interventions to include (or exclude) when reviewing the literature on 'what works' in SEL. From a practice perspective, how we define and understand SEL influences the kinds of activities we undertake with children and young people. Finally, the values and assumptions underlying SEL require critical scrutiny. These are all crucial considerations, hence it is worth spending time exploring this topic.

The prevailing definition of SEL

I have chosen to adopt the definition of SEL provided by CASEL for a number of reasons. Firstly, as we will see in the next chapter, it was members of what is now CASEL who first coined the term (Merrell and Gueldner, 2010). Secondly, CASEL are arguably the largest and most influential organisation working in this field. They define SEL as

> a process for helping children and even adults develop the fundamental skills for life effectiveness. SEL teaches the skills we all need to handle ourselves, our relationships and our work effectively and ethically. These skills include recognising and managing our emotions, developing caring and concern for others, establishing positive relationships, making responsible decisions, and handling challenging situations constructively and ethically. They are the skills that allow children to calm themselves when angry, make friends, resolve conflicts respectfully, and make ethical and safe choices. (http://www.casel.org)

There are several key elements in this definition. We will address each in turn. Firstly, SEL is a *process*. This suggests an explicit course of action, a method or practice, in which schools engage. How is this process best managed? In some of the broader SEL discourse (e.g. Elbertson et al., 2010), the word 'programming' is used, emphasising clearly the prioritisation of explicit, formal teaching of social-emotional skills, and distinguishing SEL from broader educational and social practices that might implicitly encourage the development of such competencies (for example, the socialisation of emotions in everyday adult–child interactions – Saarni, 1999). In SEL, the emphasis is on the *taught* first and foremost, with the *caught* a secondary consideration. This is demonstrated clearly in a recent CASEL publication: 'CASEL's goal is for every child to receive evidence-based *instruction* [my emphasis] in social and emotional learning' (Dusenbury et al., 2011: 2).

Craig (2007) takes issue with this, cautioning that a systematic and programmatic approach to the development of social and emotional competence in children and young people will mean that their emotional lives inevitably become the focus of checklists and assessments. Watson et al. (2012) concur, citing the 50 'learning outcomes' of the social and emotional aspects of learning (SEAL) programme in England as evidence of an attempt to apply an objective list theory to subjective emotional experience. In both cases, the authors' concerns centre on what they see as the inevitable progression from checklists to formal targets, which in turn lead to social control and compliance; effectively, SEL programmes provide a 'model' of how to think, feel and behave to which children are taught to conform (Craig, 2007). The counter to these arguments is that taking an outcomes/standards-based approach is the most effective means to secure action in an education system where this is the dominant precept – that is, what gets assessed gets attention (Dusenbury et al., 2011; Greenberg, 2010).

Critics have cited a number of other problematic assumptions in the call for explicit instruction in social and emotional skills. Craig (2007), for example, suggests that contrary to its positive intentions, SEL actually promotes a deficit model of children and young people because it gives them the message that they all need to be taught about feelings and relationships in order to function properly. Similarly, Ecclestone suggests that the growing acceptance of the need for SEL to be taught reflects a 'deeper cultural shift towards pessimistic images of people's resilience and agency' (2007: 465). Furthermore, it is seen by some as an attempt to undermine the cognitive and academic functions of education. Furedi (2009) argues this point strongly:

> Supporters of therapeutic education implicitly embrace a dogmatic counter-position of emotion to intellect. The construction of a distinct domain of emotional education is often justified on the grounds that it broadens out the classroom experience. However, the turn towards the therapeutic school is influenced by disenchantment with the purpose and effectiveness of an intellectually oriented curriculum. Supporters of the therapeutic turn often communicate an anti-academic sensibility. This sentiment is frequently shown through their self-conscious subordination of the acquisition of knowledge to the internalisation of emotional skills. (p. 170)

SEL proponents would probably accept Furedi's point (if not his tone) regarding their underlying disenfranchisement with a rationalist/technicist model of education. Indeed, much of the discourse in this area makes reference to concerns about a narrowly focused, subject-based, test-driven curriculum (see, for example, Sharp, 2000). However, from their perspective, the social-emotional and academic/cognitive are intimately intertwined rather than in opposition (Diamond, 2010). Indeed, this very notion is embodied in the name 'CASEL' – the Collaborative for *Academic*, Social and Emotional Learning. That children's social and emotional functioning underpins their academic success is also a key tenet of the SEL logic model that will be explored later in this chapter.

 Points for Reflection

- How are SEL and academic progress related? Is it possible to promote the latter without paying attention to the former?

The universalist approach (and its potential problems)

The second important component of this definition is its emphasis on the universal nature of SEL instruction – this is something *we all need*. There are a number of reasons why proponents advocate SEL instruction for all children as opposed to those at risk of (or already) experiencing difficulties. The most fundamental of these is based upon the idiom 'an ounce of prevention is worth a pound of cure'. This notion has a clear intuitive appeal – by providing SEL instruction to all children and young people, we can effectively immunise them from mental health difficulties and other negative outcomes (Merrell and Gueldner, 2010). In theory, such a system would also be cheaper to implement since it would avoid the costly screening procedures needed to identify those at risk (which, of course, may miss some children in need of targeted support) and the use of highly trained professionals that are often required to deliver targeted interventions (McLaughlin, 2011). As a result, universal preventive approaches are considered to be more sustainable. Finally, because universal approaches by definition include all children, their potential for stigmatising participants is reduced (Greenberg, 2010) and they therefore align better with the principles of inclusive education.

However, the universalist approach to SEL embodied in the CASEL definition also carries some drawbacks. Chief among these is that because the prevalence of mental health difficulties is relatively low (Green et al., 2005), much of the effort expended in universal programmes is on children who are unlikely to develop difficulties anyway. Furthermore, the relatively 'light touch' approach to intervention (in terms of intensity and duration) taken may not be sufficient to impact upon outcomes for those children who *are* at risk (Greenberg, 2010). A balance between universal (for everyone), targeted (for those considered to be at risk) and indicated (for those already experiencing difficulties) interventions is therefore typically recommended (Wells et al., 2003). However, there has been only limited study of how these different 'tiers' of intervention interact with one another, and the research that has been conducted has produced equivocal results. For example, Sheffield et al.'s randomised controlled trial (2006) examined the impact of universal, indicated and combined universal *plus* indicated cognitive-behavioural interventions among adolescents, compared to a 'usual practice' control group. They found no benefit in any of the three intervention conditions among at risk *or* the general population of students on a range of measures relating to mental health, coping skills and social adjustment. Given the predominance of the tiered approach, more research in this area should be a priority.

 Points for Reflection

- If targeted/indicated interventions are always needed to supplement universal programmes, does this fundamentally challenge the extent to which the latter can be considered successful in helping children who are 'at risk'?

What is the nature of the skills imparted through SEL?

A third element for us to consider in examining what we mean by SEL is the nature/content of the social and emotional skills themselves. The work of contemporary developmental psychologists is useful here. In thematically analysing a range of perspectives on SEL (including the CASEL definition), Denham and Brown (2010) provide a useful taxonomy, which at the broadest level distinguishes between emotional competence skills and relational/pro-social skills. Emotional competence skills comprise self-awareness, self-regulation and social awareness. Relational/pro-social skills comprise relationship skills and responsible decision-making. Saarni's (1999) influential model of emotional development follows similar lines, proposing eight key skills of emotional competence, as follows:

1. Awareness of one's emotional state and motivations, for example knowing when one is becoming angry and what may have triggered this.
2. The ability to identify and understand emotions in others, such as knowing when someone is feeling happy.
3. The ability to articulate emotional language, for example being able to state clearly and accurately how one is feeling.
4. The capacity for empathic involvement, that is feeling *with* others (e.g. seeing someone upset makes us also feel sadness).
5. Understanding that internal emotional experience and external emotional expression may be incongruent, for example inhibiting one's joy at being dealt a royal flush in poker (the eponymous 'poker face').
6. Coping with aversive emotions and stressful situations, that is being 'stress hardy' and able to 'roll with the punches'.
7. Understanding emotional communication within relationships, in other words knowing that our emotion-related behaviour and understanding underpins our relationships with others.
8. Emotional self-efficacy, viewing ourselves as 'feeling the way we want to feel' and, perhaps more broadly, that we are able to use our emotional competence to produce adaptive outcomes.

Key to both models is that they are *developmental* in nature. Weare (2004) makes the important point that the lists and taxonomies of social and emotional skills that are infused throughout the SEL literature can imply that 'exist all at one level' (p. 21), when in fact they develop over time. So, we would expect greater self-regulatory capacity in a child of 13 than in a toddler – although I am informed by parents of teenagers that this is not always the case! These developmental sequences emerge as a function of both endogenous (internal) and exogenous (external) factors, and the interaction between the two. In support of this, Goldsmith et al. (2008) note that the emergence of skills involved in decoding and conveying emotional signals are dependent both upon the child's social environment (which of courses dictates the kind of emotional experiences they are exposed to) and the growth of specific neural substrates, but importantly that the two influence one another. (For example, a child's temperament, largely internally derived, may influence the response behaviour of care givers in his or her immediate social environment, which in turn may feedback into the growth patterns of neural systems.)

From the point of view of SEL, the developmental nature of social and emotional competence means that for programmes to be appropriate (and, presumably, effective), their content should be *developmentally aligned and sequenced* – that is, in sync with norms of the different domains of competence for the age group(s) in question, and designed in such a way that the content unfolds in line with typical developmental patterns. Assuming that this is the case, an interesting question is raised about the level of the instruction – do we 'teach, model, practise and apply' (Durlak et al., 2011) social and emotional skills that are already part of most children's repertoires (thereby merely reinforcing and consolidating existing knowledge, understanding and behavioural response patterns), or use SEL instruction to advance these repertoires by teaching more sophisticated concepts that may be just beyond their immediate understanding?

A fourth principal component of the SEL definition is the assumption of unanimity in the model of emotions that is presented through the various skills cited (see above). This belies the broad range of cultural differences in emotional experience and expression that have been consistently established (Hoffman, 2009). Hoffman cites the emphasis on talking about or otherwise articulating emotions inherent in SEL as reflecting the cultural preferences of white, middle-class America, and failing to address the fact that in many other cultures, a more stoic model of self-expression is valued. Saarni (1999) concurs, noting the 'Western cultural bias' inherent in models of emotional development, and provides extensive and wide-ranging examples of cultural variations for each of the eight core skills highlighted above. Weare (2004) goes further, questioning the incontrovertibility of any attempt to set parameters on what skills are to be valued: 'Deciding what goes on a list of emotional and social competences cannot be value-free, culture-free or an apolitical exercise' (p. 19). In fairness, there is an acknowledgement of these kinds of issues in some of the SEL literature (e.g. Denham and Weissberg, 2004), but there is much more work to be done in order to develop a framework for SEL that is appropriately culture-sensitive.

〰️   **Points for Reflection**

- Is it possible to have a definition of SEL that is truly sensitive to cultural variation and individual differences?

In summary, the prevailing definition provided by CASEL provides a useful framework for understanding the concept of SEL. However, when considered from a critical perspective, it also carries with it a number of assumptions, values and problematic issues pertaining to the nature and functions of schooling and the emotional lives of children and young people. Chief among these are the assumed need for explicit instruction in social and emotional competence, the universality of this need, and the explication of a model of emotion that does not take into account cultural differences in the experience and expression of emotion. These issues bring forth broader questions about the relationship between social-emotional and cognitive-academic aspects of schooling.

The broader discourse – diversity or dilution?

The broader discourse around SEL takes the essence of the concept discussed above and adapts, modifies and dilutes it to the point at which – in some instances – it can be something qualitatively different. Indeed, in a certain sense, SEL has arguably become a synonym for any positive or desirable aspect of education that is outside of the basic academic curriculum. This is one of several interesting parallels that it shares with its conceptual forebear, emotional intelligence (EI), whose meaning has similarly been modified in some sections of the literature to describe 'all those positive qualities that are not IQ' (Matthews et al., 2004: 180).

As the SEL movement has gathered pace, it has subsumed a bewildering array of different definitions and related terms. Merrell and Gueldner (2010) suggest that 'SEL both incorporates and broadens several areas of focus . . . including *social competence training, positive youth development, violence prevention, character education, primary prevention, mental health promotion*, and others' (p. 6). Similarly, Hoffman (2009) notes that SEL is used as an umbrella term that incorporates a wide variety of programmes, including those noted above and adding *conflict resolution* and *juvenile justice* approaches. To this conceptual 'smorgasbord' we can add *emotional literacy* (Weare,

2004) and, of course, *emotional intelligence* (Goleman, 1996). The 'loose framing' of SEL impacts upon practices in the field of study that affect conceptual rigour. For example, in Durlak et al.'s (2011) meta-analysis, an intervention only needed to be seen to address one of the authors' five key competencies (these were the same as those proposed by Denham and Brown (2010) above) in order to be included, introducing considerable variability and ambiguity that belies the use of a single descriptive term (e.g. 'SEL programmes').

Why is it important to examine the conceptual inconsistency inherent in the broader discourse? Some authors argue that points of variance and even disagreement are of no consequence, particularly in relation to the practice of SEL in schools (Merrell and Gueldner, 2010). An important reason for setting clear parameters with regard to what SEL is (and is not) and how it relates to other areas of focus is to ensure conceptual clarity. The protean quality ascribed to SEL in the current discourse in the field places it in danger – like EI before it – of becoming 'bereft of any conceptual meaning' (Zeidner et al., 2002: 215). Essentially, the broader the term 'SEL' becomes, the less utility it has, as it enables the gradual incorporation of increasingly diverse sources of evidence about programmes that bear less and less resemblance to any fundamental concept of social and/or emotional competence, at least as it is articulated and understood by developmental psychologists (e.g. Saarni, 1999).

The lack of conceptual clarity also makes a common understanding nigh impossible. Thus two people could both have equally valid and yet completely different ideas about what is meant by SEL, and thus how it might be theorised, researched and practised in school settings. This ambiguity can also create issues when making recommendations for policy and practice from research findings, because it creates space for evidence for one approach to be 'borrowed' and used to advocate another, potentially very different approach (Humphrey, 2009).

The mutable nature of SEL also influences its enactment in schools, because it has allowed the introduction of practices that are conducted 'in the name of' SEL but which may have little direct relevance to the concept, and in some cases are completely spurious. For example, Zeidner et al. (2002) observe that some school-based SEL interventions actually contain little in the way of *social* and/or *emotional* content. In some cases, this has led to an 'anything goes' model – with, for example, some children being taught that their bodies have seven 'energy centres', each with a different colour, as part of the SEAL programme in England (BBC, 2011), or indeed children participating in 'Cheryl Cole lessons' (Henry, 2011) as part of attempts to develop their emotional literacy.

Mapping SEL and associated concepts

As noted above, setting the parameters of SEL and exploring the areas of convergence and divergence with related concepts is an important task for both theoretical and practical reasons. In an attempt to provide some lucidity in light of the issues outlined above, I have developed a conceptual map of SEL and related terms (see Figure 2.1). In truth, this was created as a means to clarify my own understanding of what SEL is and how it links with related areas, but I hope it is also of use to the readership of this book. It should be noted from the outset that this is by no means a definitive or completely comprehensive model – rather, it is a work in progress that attempts to simplify a confusing field.

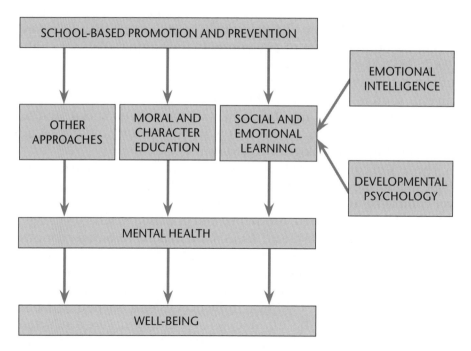

Figure 2.1   A concept map of SEL and related terms

At the top of the map – and at the broadest level, conceptually speaking – is the field of school-based prevention. This field is concerned with the *prevention* of negative outcomes (such as mental health disorders) and the *promotion* of positive attributes and competencies (such as social skills) through universal interventions in schools (see Chapter 3) (Weisz et al., 2005). Prevention and promotion operate in a state of continuous interaction. They are 'two sides of the same coin'. Thus programmes that seek to promote positive attributes and competencies in children and young people are, in doing so, also working to prevent negative outcomes, and vice versa. Indeed, this is often how they are operationalised – so, for example, many programmes that seek to promote social, emotional and cognitive competence are also effective in reducing negative outcomes such as alcohol use and violence (National Research Council and Institute of Medicine, 2009). As we will see later, this is a key tenet of the SEL logic model.

Within the prevention and promotion field there are a variety of distinct but related approaches that may be applied in schools. These include SEL, moral and character education, and those with a more specific remit (such as programmes designed to tackle a specific issue, such as substance abuse prevention or school transition). Although there may be shared ground between these, I would argue that they are distinct at the conceptual level.

Moral and character education focuses on the teaching of moral and ethical values (and, latterly, ways of behaving) based around concepts such as respect, justice, honesty and integrity (Elias, 2009), whose aim is to help children grow into good citizens (Kohn, 1997). Aspects of character education are often found in the general SEL discourse. Indeed, some authors consider it to be paramount, explicitly placing it at the forefront of their writing. Elias (2009), for example, refers to 'social, emotional and character development' (SECD) as opposed to SEL. Similarly, Cohen (2006) refers to 'social, emotional, ethical and academic education' (SEEAE). Even the aforementioned CASEL definition makes reference to 'ethics' three times.

However, the infusion of aspects of character education in SEL imposes a set of values and assumptions about what it means to be 'ethical' in our behaviour. Kohn (1997), for example, suggests that character education 'rests on three ideological legs: behaviourism, conservatism and religion' (p. 436). In my view, this means that it is distinct from 'pure' SEL as drawn from models of emotional intelligence and/or developmental psychological theory. The various social and emotional skills noted earlier in this chapter can be practised independently of ethical integrity or moral influence.

For example, children acquire increasingly sophisticated emotional understanding during the course of their development, but they need not always apply this understanding in a manner that is consistent with the moral or ethical values espoused through character education

– thus, good character is not necessarily synonymous with high levels of social and emotional competence (Mayer and Cobb, 2000). Indeed, Pellegrini and Long (2002) have suggested that manipulating other children may be one way in which youngsters manage relationships as they make sense of evolving social roles during the transition from childhood to adolescence. A relationship between emotional competence and Machiavellianism has also been proposed in adults, although research findings remain inconclusive to date (Austin et al., 2007).

The distinction between SEL and character education can also be seen in some of the cultural variation evident in approaches taken around the world. For example, in the USA, there has arguably been a much stronger focus on the infusion of character and moral education into SEL than in other countries (see Chapter 4).

The backbone of SEL

SEL stands distinct from these other prevention and promotion approaches in the concept map as the *application to education of emotional intelligence theory and research* (Hoffman, 2009) and *developmental psychological models of social and emotional competence* (Denham and Brown, 2010). These two substantive areas of theory and research provide the 'backbone' of SEL in terms of their historical influence on the emergence of the field (see Chapter 3) and in the core taxonomy of social and emotional competencies expressed in each. The influence of developmental psychological models is particularly important since it brings to bear theory and research pertaining to how these competencies emerge and interact during the course of children's development – thus avoiding the imposition of a 'rational adult' model of competence (Weare, 2004).

Emotional intelligence (along with its common alias, emotional literacy) theory and research provides the 'integrative concept' of SEL (Elias, 1997). EI gained widespread public attention following the publication of Goleman's (1996) book on the subject, but its academic roots extend much further back, arguably to Thorndike's work on social intelligence in the early part of the last century. However, the EI model that has been most influential in the SEL field has been the one published by Salovey and Mayer (1990), in which it is defined as 'the capacity to process emotional information accurately and efficiently, including the capacity to perceive, assimilate, understand, and manage emotion' (Mayer and Cobb, 2000: 165). Salovey and

Mayer's original model (ibid.) integrates four specific emotion-related abilities: (a) the accurate perception of emotions; (b) using emotions to facilitate thought; (c) knowledge and understanding of emotions; and (d) the management or regulation of emotions.

Salovey and Mayer's EI model has stood up to empirical scrutiny (Mayer et al., 2008). However, in much the same way as SEL, as EI has become more popular, the concept has become diluted. Over a decade ago, Mayer and Cobb (2000) cautioned that it had become 'a catchphrase for anything that involved motivation, emotion, or good character' (p. 170). Subsequent models and definitions of EI capture this conceptual confusion well. For example, Petrides and Furnham's (2001) definition of 'trait' EI covers an astonishing 15 different facets: adaptability, low impulsiveness, self-esteem, self-motivation, stress management, trait happiness, trait optimism, assertiveness, relationship skills, social competence, trait empathy, emotional expression, emotional management, emotional perception and emotional regulation.

Mental health and well-being

Downstream of SEL in the concept map are the terms *mental health* and *well-being*. I use the term 'downstream' to imply that both mental health and the broader notion of well-being are considered to be a consequence of (or follow on from) SEL. For example, Weare and Markham (2005) describe social and emotional competencies as 'the skills . . . that underlie mental health' (p. 120). Denham et al. (2009) concur, suggesting that failure to meet developmental milestones in the different domains of intra- and interpersonal competence lead to an increased risk of psychopathology. Empirical evidence would appear to support these assertions, as empathy (e.g. Green et al., 2005), self-awareness (e.g. Posse et al., 2002), self-regulation (e.g. Gross and Muñoz, 1995) and social skills (e.g. Rae-Grant et al., 1989) have each been highlighted as protective factors for mental health disorders. Some of our own research at Manchester has suggested that this protective role for such social and emotional competencies may be in moderating the relationship between chronic stressors (e.g. family dysfunction, negative life events, socio-economic adversity) and mental health outcomes (Davis and Humphrey, 2012b).

However, as is the emerging pattern in this section of the chapter, these terms are bedevilled by incoherence. In relation to *mental health*, a key issue has been how to operationalise the relationship between wellness and illness (Shucksmith et al., 2009). Is mental health simply the absence of mental health difficulties, or is it something more? Are they two ends of the same continuum?

 Points for Reflection

- What does it mean to be mentally healthy?

Assessment and measurement practices in this area have not helped, taking a predominantly clinical, illness-based focus at the expense of health (see Johnston and Gowers' (2005) review of the most commonly used instruments in UK Child and Adolescent Mental Health Services for evidence of this). It is only relatively recently that measures of 'positive' mental health have begun to emerge (e.g. the Warwick-Edinburgh Mental Wellbeing Scale – Clarke et al., 2010). A useful 'dual focus' (in the sense of considering both wellness and illness) definition is provided by Adi et al. (2007), who see mental health as:

- *emotional health* – being happy and confident, not depressed and anxious;

- *psychological health* – being resilient and autonomous;

- *social/relational health* – having good relationships with others, and not behaving in a way that can cause them harm, such as bullying.

Mental health forms part of the much broader term of *well-being*, which is perhaps the most amorphous and loosely defined of all of those under consideration in the current chapter. Statham and Chase (2010) suggest that it most broadly refers to quality of life. This might then include factors such as the experience of poverty and deprivation, physical health, subjective well-being and mental health, education, housing, use of time and space, crime and so on (Bradshaw, 2011). However, as Eraut and Whiting (2008) convincingly argue, well-being has a somewhat 'holographic' quality – that is, different meanings are projected by different individuals, and what is meant depends entirely on the perspective taken, the only commonality being that it is considered a good thing. 'Well-being' is also readily applied as a suffix to existing terms – for example, 'social and emotional well-being' is often used as a synonym for mental health.

How does SEL work? An analysis of the logic model

Having (hopefully!) established what we mean by SEL, the next logical step is to explore and analyse the processes by which it is theorised to bring about the range of positive outcomes that are claimed. The SEL logic model is a crucial aspect of the overall picture. Without it, we are effectively left with a 'black box' view. That is, we would know the inputs (e.g. SEL programme X) and the outputs (e.g. outcome Y), but have no idea how they related to one another, and indeed whether there are any mediating factors or variables. Thus a logic model 'describes the sequence of events for bringing about change by synthesizing the main program elements into a picture of how the program is supposed to work' (Centers for Disease Control and Prevention, 1999: 9). Logic models – which are also sometimes referred to as chains of reasoning or theories of action (Mclaughlin and Jordan, 1999) – are therefore an essential component of programme descriptions. They allow developers to clarify the strategy of a given intervention, reveal assumptions about conditions for programme effectiveness, provide a frame of reference for evaluation, and can strengthen claims about causality (Centers for Disease Control and Prevention, 1999).

The CASEL logic model (CASEL, 2007) describes the processes by which SEL works to produce a range of positive outcomes for students. It may be considered a 'meta' logic model since it describes a series of processes that may be generalised to SEL interventions at large rather than relating to a specific programme (as is typically the case in the development of logic models). It should also be noted that several well known SEL programmes, such as the PATHS curriculum, have their own theory of action or logic model, which may have somewhat different foci to the general model produced by CASEL. For example, the PATHS logic model focuses on the neurocognitive processes involved in the promotion of social competence (Riggs et al., 2006). The CASEL logic model is shown in Figure 2.2.

The fundamental tenets of the CASEL SEL logic model are as follows. Firstly, it proposes that SEL interventions do two main things – firstly, they create school and classroom climates that are well-managed and participatory, and in which students feels safe and cared for. At the same time, they provide explicit instruction in the development of social and emotional competence (e.g. self-awareness, relationship skills). An important early acknowledgement in CASEL's description of the SEL logic model is that 'few SEL programs accomplish all of these objectives. Instead, schools typically combine programs with strengths in one area or the other to achieve the full benefits of SEL programming' (CASEL, 2007: 1). It is therefore unsurprising that Zins

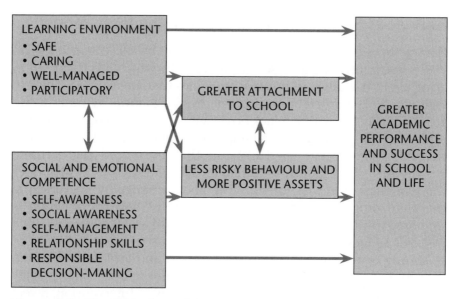

Figure 2.2   The SEL logic model

Safe and Sound: An Educational Leader's Guide to Evidence-Based Social and Emotional Learning (SEL) Programs. Chicago: Collaborative for Academic, Social, and Emotional Learning (CASEL), 2003. Used with permission of the authors.

et al. (2004) reported that schools in the US implement a median of *14* different approaches. The lack of truly comprehensive SEL interventions is further evidenced in reviews of the literature, which routinely only identify a handful of interventions that promote dual foci on both the environment/ethos and a taught curriculum, with most opting to focus almost exclusively on the latter (Adi et al., 2007; Blank et al., 2010). Given that this is the case, an immediate concern arises – if both aspects of SEL are fundamental cornerstones of the logic model, does this mean that those interventions which focus primarily on a taught curriculum (or, indeed, on the school environment/ethos) are likely to yield less beneficial effects? The evidence does not seem to suggest that this is the case – as noted elsewhere, two recent major meta-analyses found no advantage of multi-component approaches when compared to those with a single component (Durlak et al., 2011; Wilson and Lipsey, 2007).

Direct links between SEL and school outcomes

The second assertion of the logic model is that the two proposed core elements of SEL programmes have both direct and indirect effects on children's school and life outcomes. In terms of direct links, the rationale is captured eloquently by Zins et al. (2004): 'Schools are social places and learning is a social process. Students do not learn alone but rather in collaboration with their teachers, in the company of their peers, and with the support of their families' (p. 3). Hence, SEL improves students' school outcomes because it enables them to work better with others. This proposal has an intuitive logic to it that will surely resonate with anyone who has worked in and around schools – but what does the research tell us? Here we may draw evidence from studies that have evaluated the effects of SEL programmes on school outcomes, and also those that use a longitudinal, natural variation framework in order to ascertain the temporal relations between social-emotional and academic domains.

In terms of evaluation studies, we have already seen that Durlak et al.'s (2011) recent meta-analysis found effects equivalent to an 11 percentile point increase in children's academic scores as a result of participating in an SEL programme. Data from individual studies cited by CASEL (2007) provide similarly appealing findings. For example, the various empirical investigations of the High/Scope pre-school curriculum, 'designed to foster social-emotional competence' (CASEL, 2007: 5), show impressive outcomes in a variety of salient domains (e.g. educational achievement, economic performance, participation in crime), with some effects still evident at age 40 (Schweinhart et al., 2005). However, inspection of High/Scope reveals it to be much more than a programme designed to promote SEL; it is in fact a comprehensive educational approach based around active participatory learning, wherein the emphasis is on providing direct, hands-on learning experiences for young children. Indeed, social and emotional development is just one of eight key content areas of High/Scope, which also includes language and literacy, maths, science and social studies. Hence, it is perhaps misleading to attribute the impressive academic and other benefits of High/Scope and programmes like it solely to the effects of the SEL component.

Some other studies focusing on 'pure' SEL programmes have provided evidence for the direct links asserted in the logic model, but with differential effects for particular sub-groups of children. For example, Ashdown and Bernard's (2011) evaluation of the 'You Can Do It!' SEL curriculum in Australia demonstrated positive effects on literacy, but only for children with low reading levels at the beginning of the study. Hence, as noted elsewhere in this text, the benefits of SEL may not be as universal as is implied in the discourse. The issue of these 'differential benefits' will be discussed in more depth in Chapter 7.

Studies using a longitudinal, natural variation framework add to the rather confusing picture. Two recent analyses (Duncan et al., 2007; Romano et al., 2010) conducted using large American, Canadian and British datasets found *no* significant links between social and emotional competence and later academic achievement in school-aged children after controlling for the influence of cognitive (e.g. attention) and academic (e.g. reading, maths) skills. However, in contrast, Petrides et al.'s (2004) research found that trait emotional intelligence (akin to self-reported social and emotional competence – see Chapter 5) moderated the effects of cognitive ability on overall academic performance in English adolescents, and was directly inversely linked to the likelihood of truancy and expulsion from school.

Indirect links between SEL and school outcomes

The other proposed method through which SEL improves school outcomes in the logic model is via its mediating/moderating influence on students' attachment to school and their likelihood of engaging in risky and/or adaptive behaviour, both of which in turn influence subsequent academic performance. In terms of the first step, there is again evidence from the recent meta-analysis, with SEL interventions yielding effects on students' attitudes to themselves and school of a similar magnitude to the findings for academic performance noted above (Durlak et al., 2011). Longitudinal research has been supportive of the proposed link, with school climate influencing middle-school students' vulnerability to psychopathology (Kuperminc et al., 2001). Similarly, perceptions of school climate among high-school students have been demonstrated to affect their endorsement of positive attitudes towards help seeking for bullying and threats of violence (Eliot et al., 2010).

The second step in the indirect effects element of the logic model proposes a link between students' attachment to school, their likelihood of engaging in risky and/or adaptive behaviour and subsequent academic performance. This proposed link is likely to resonate strongly with most educators, but there is also clear empirical support. So, for example, the recent National Youth Risk Behavior Survey found a clear negative association between engagement in health-risk behaviours (e.g. using alcohol, carrying a weapon) and academic achievement among adolescents in the United States, even after controlling for a range of other influential factors (e.g. sex, ethnicity) (US Department of Health and Human Services, 2010). However, it should be noted that this research was cross-sectional in nature and also relied on students' self-report of their academic progress. For a more robust demonstration of the links proposed in this stage of the logic model, we can turn to Stewart's (2007) longitudinal research, which highlighted clear links between students' attachment and commitment to school and their subsequent academic achievement. Interestingly, this study also found that school cohesion (e.g. more positive interactions and trust between students and teachers) was also associated with academic progress.

In summary, the SEL logic model carries a great deal of intuitive appeal and there is empirical support for the various proposed pathways from a range of studies. However, some of the evidence suggests that SEL may actually play a relatively small role in a much larger picture (e.g. the High/Scope study), and indeed some studies fail to provide any support for the model (e.g. Duncan et al., 2007). One crucial issue here is the amount of variation in children's academic success that is uniquely attributable to SEL. Even among studies that provide robust evidence for some of the proposed links in the model, analyses suggest a relatively small, incremental contribution (e.g. Petrides et al., 2004). The issue of 'causal ordering' (that is, whether x causes y, or whether y causes x) also warrants further attention. For example, Bryant and Schulenberg's (2003) six-year longitudinal study provided evidence for the influence of academic achievement on later risky behaviour (in this case, substance abuse), suggesting that, at the very least, there may be 'reciprocal' rather than 'one-way' cause-effect relationships at play. Finally, given that the logic model is intended to provide an explanation of how SEL programmes influence success in school, a critical missed opportunity thus far is the failure of most SEL evaluation studies to actually assess temporal relations between social and emotional skill development and academic outcome variables (Durlak et al., 2011).

 ## Further Reading

Hoffman, D. M. (2009) 'Reflecting on social emotional learning: a critical perspective on trends in the United States', *Review of Educational Research*, 79: 533–56.

Zins, J. E., Bloodworth, M. R., Weissberg, R. P. and Walberg, H. J. (2007). 'The scientific base linking social and emotional learning to school success', *Journal of Educational and Psychological Consultation*, 17: 191–210.

3

Origins and influences

Overview

The aim of this chapter is to chart and discuss the origins of and influences on the field of SEL. In doing so we will consider the history of emotions in education, the various conceptualisations of social, emotional and multiple intelligences, progressive education, notions of risk, protection and resilience, the field of prevention, the self-esteem movement, the youth in crisis metaphor and the political and economic forces that have driven the development of SEL.

Key Points

*   Consideration of affective experience in education is nothing new, but recent decades have seen a change in the importance attributed to the role of emotions in learning.
*   Emotional intelligence is the integrative concept of SEL, and its populist version (e.g. Goleman, 1996) has fuelled the rapid growth of the field.
*   SEL can be seen as a 'progeny' of the self-esteem movement.
*   The rationale for SEL is influenced by the discourses of youth in crisis and risk, protection and resilience, but these have been accepted somewhat uncritically.

- The economic costs of mental health problems and their consequences provide a powerful driver for SEL.
- Educational policy has played a somewhat contradictory role in the development of SEL. Government acts and initiatives that might promote growth and opportunity for SEL are often stifled by a more dominant, narrowly focused agenda of academic standards.

The historical roots of SEL

The phrase 'social and emotional learning' is believed to have first been coined during early meetings of what would become CASEL in 1993 (CASEL, 2004). However, work on the social and emotional aspects of education has been carried out for a much longer period of time. The ideas and values underpinning SEL stretch back thousands of years. For example, the Greek philosopher Aristotle spoke of the importance of anger management (Weare, 2004). Similarly, when Plato wrote about education in *The Republic*, he emphasised the need for a curriculum that included attention to personal and social facets as well as academic subjects. Indeed, throughout history many key thinkers have made reference to the importance of emotions in their treatises on human experience, often in discussions about education and learning (see the Centre for the History of Emotions at http://www.qmul.ac.uk/emotions).

Dixon (2012) provides insights into the more recent history of 'educating the emotions', charting the growing influence attributed to this aspect of development throughout and beyond the nineteenth century. He cites an 1829 edition of the *Quarterly Review*, which stated, 'the first 8 to 10 years of life should be devoted to the education of the heart . . . rather than to the acquirement of what is usually termed knowledge' (p. 2), and in doing so provides clear evidence that even nearly two centuries ago, the affective domain was a consideration in education.

Progressive education

Around the end of the nineteenth century, the progressive education movement, led by John Dewey, laid further foundations for the move towards a social and emotional model of education. In doing so, the seeds were sown for what would eventually become known as SEL. Progressive education is fundamentally concerned with providing an alternative to test-focused instruction and the traditional academic curriclum (Hayes, 2006). It incorporates a strong emphasis on experiential learning, critical thinking and problem-solving. In terms of the origins of SEL, there is also a strong emphasis on social skills, collaboration and cooperation. Much of what Dewey in particular wrote resonates strongly with the fundamental principles of SEL outlined in the previous chapter, including the belief that 'the only true education comes through the stimulation of the child's powers by the demands of the social situation in which he finds himself' (Dewey, 1897: 77). Progressive education methods such as experiential learning can be seen in most schools to this day, although they are rarely referred to as such, presumably because we assume that pedagogy has already progressed and they are now 'standard' teaching practice.

The interplay between emotions and reason

So in its essence, SEL is certainly not a 'new' idea. But historically, the affective aspects of human experience have not been as revered as they are today. As Weare (2004) suggests, 'Society has traditionally been frightened of emotion' (p. ix). Much of this fear comes from the perceived conflict between emotion/affect and reason/rationality. Rationality, characterised by conformity with reason, order and structure, testability and simplicity, was seen as being undermined by emotions, particularly in relation to decision-making (Humphrey et al., 2007). Indeed, Plato wrote of emotion and reason as being like two horses pulling us in opposite directions. Exceptions to this view were rare. However, one notable voice of insurgence was nineteenth-century philosopher John Stuart Mill, who felt that educating the emotions and the intellect could and should go hand in hand (Dixon, 2012). The predominance of rationality meant that, until relatively recently, emotions and emotional experience were placed in an inferior position to cognition. What we know now, of course, is that the view of emotion and reason as diametrically opposed is too simplistic, and that, 'emotions . . . are profoundly intertwined with thought' (Immordino-Yang and Damasio, 2007: 4).

Points for Reflection

- Why might emotion and reason have traditionally been viewed as diametric opposites?

The influence of social, emotional and multiple intelligences

The concept of cognitive intelligence predominated for a large part of the last century, influenced by the work of Binet and Burt among others. In its earliest and most narrow conceptualisations, intelligence sat well alongside a rationalist model of schooling, being focused around individuals' planning, reasoning, judgement, memory and other aspects of cognitive (as opposed to affective) processing. Although some early intelligence theorists such as Thorndike (Thorndike and Stein, 1937) provided broader parameters for what might constitute intelligence (e.g. 'social intelligence'), it was not really until the publication of Howard Gardner's theory of multiple intelligences (Gardner, 1983), and subsequently Salovey and Mayer's (1990) and Goleman's (1996) work on emotional intelligence, that such ideas began to receive widespread attention.

Howard Gardner (1983) proposed that intelligence could be thought of in terms of seven distinct capacities: logical-mathematical, spatial, linguistic, musical, bodily-kinesthetic, intrapersonal and interpersonal. In a later revision of his theory, Gardner combined intrapersonal and interpersonal intelligences, perhaps influenced by ongoing work on emotional intelligence (e.g. Salovey and Mayer, 1990 onwards). Since then, he has proposed a variety of other forms, including naturalistic intelligence, existential intelligence, mental searchlight intelligence and laser intelligence (Waterhouse, 2006). In parallel to this, emotional intelligence theorists such as Salovey, Mayer, Bar-On and others have continued to develop ideas about this more specific construct (Mayer et al., 2008) (see Chapter 2). Crucially, Goleman's (1996 onwards) work has served to bring it to the attention of the general public.

The influence of social, emotional and multiple intelligences on the development and popularisation of SEL is clearly evident. As noted in the Chapter 2, EI provides the 'organising idea' of SEL. However, it has also served several other important functions. Firstly, it could be argued that the use of the word 'intelligence' in discourse has helped to give SEL added legitimacy and status among educators. This is despite the fact that in academic circles the notion of EI as a genuine form of intelligence continues to be hotly debated (see, for example, Matthews et al., 2004). Secondly, the popularisation of EI through Daniel Goleman's work provided a useful 'hook' because of its familiarity. In my experience, few teachers have heard of Salovey and Mayer, but many more know about Goleman. As Sternberg (2002) states, his work 'stirred the imaginations of many people' (p. xii). A clear example of this can be seen in the SEAL programme in England, where Goleman is cited liberally in the guidance for schools and, indeed, his typology of EI serves as a central framework. Finally, the EI framework holds intrinsic appeal to educators dissatisfied with the status and priority afforded to cognitive ability and testing (Sharp, 2000), particularly given the claims initially made by Goleman, who famously asserted that EI was more predictive of key life outcomes than IQ.

 Points for Reflection

• What are the potential drawbacks of the association between SEL and populist conceptualisations of social, emotional and multiple intelligences?

The self-esteem movement

Self-esteem appears as a component in some of the models presented in the EI and SEL discourse. For example, consider the 'Good to Be Me' theme of the primary SEAL programme in England (Department for Education and Skills, 2005a). The growth of the self-esteem movement in the 1970s and 1980s also bears some striking parallels to that of the SEL field in the last two decades. Like the topic of this book, self-esteem is a concept whose shared meaning is assumed by most, when in fact there are multiple, competing ideas as to exactly what it constitutes (see Chapter 2). It is also a movement whose popularity was kick-started by the publication of a book (Nathaniel Branden's *The Psychology of Self-Esteem* (1969)) that gained widespread public attention, and made similar claims to Daniel Goleman (see above) about the importance of its central topic – namely that positive self-esteem is the key to success in life. Alongside this there was (and still is) a core body of credible theory and research, led by the likes of Herbert Marsh and Susan Harter, who make much more restrained claims about the role played by self-esteem in improving outcomes.

The idea of self-esteem needing to be explicitly taught in schools initially began to gain momentum in the state of California, set against a backdrop of growing concerns about America's youth. Authors such as Branden claimed that most, if not all, of the problems facing young people, which included mental health difficulties, substance abuse and interpersonal violence, could be attributed to low self-esteem. These and other negative outcomes are currently used as part of the rationale for SEL in the contemporary discourse (see next section). The California State Department developed a self-esteem 'taskforce' in the early 1980s at a cost of around three-quarters of a million dollars. Much of the focus of their activities was the active facilitation of self-esteem in the classroom (California Self-Esteem Taskforce, 1990). In another parallel to SEL, claims were made about how such activities would indirectly boost children's academic attainment (Baumeister, 2005). These ideas were enthusiastically embraced by many educators, who – just as has been the case with the emergence of SEL more recently – were perhaps disenfranchised with the narrow academic curriculum that they were required to teach. The movement was underpinned by a growing evidence base appearing to demonstrate the importance of self-esteem, but one that was not definitive when subjected to close analysis. Ultimately, the active teaching of self-esteem began to lose favour, particularly when research more consistently identified it as a *consequence* rather than a *cause* of children's academic attainment.

Despite the above similarities, there are also a number of lessons that have been learned from the rise and fall of the self-esteem movement. The field of SEL has arguably more actively embraced a synthesis with traditional academic instruction. It has also provided a much more credible model of change (see Chapter 2), and drawn much more effectively on educational and psychological theory in doing so. SEL is perhaps a 'bigger idea' than self-esteem in terms of its comprehensiveness and links to different aspects of human experience. Finally, despite some of the inconsistencies and flaws evident in the research base noted throughout this text, SEL has benefited from the increased quality of research in education in the last two decades. As a result of such facets, it has garnered much greater attention among educators in the United States and internationally (see Chapter 4) than the self-esteem movement ever did.

A youth in crisis

A key driver in the growth of SEL has surely been the prevalent view that the current generation of children are experiencing a profound crisis, the like of which has never been seen before (Hoffman, 2009). Indeed, this view is common to many contemporary media portrayals of young people, where they are often characterised as fragile, stressed and depressed and/or as feral, uncontrollable animals (Guldberg, 2009). However, the youth in crisis view can also be seen in the academic discourse (Lerner, 1995). Consider the following introduction to a paper on SEL: 'High stakes tests. Substance abuse. Suicide. Academic standards, Delinquency. Media and technology. Teacher retention. Interpersonal violence. Changes in families. The list of issues facing *today's* [my emphasis] educators and students is daunting' (Zins and Elias, 2007: 233). Similarly, in a recent conference on the secondary SEAL programme in England, one of the keynote speakers drew upon an account of a Holocaust survivor, which beseeched future educators to avoid producing 'learned monsters, skilled psychopaths, [and] educated Eichmanns' (Gross, 2010). Such discourse brings to mind images of a youth that are collectively broken in some way and need to be fixed (Watson et al., 2012).

In the last few years in the United Kingdom, the youth in crisis discourse has focused on the rather elusive concept of 'well-being' (see Chapter 2), triggered primarily by a widely reported and rather uncritically accepted piece of international comparative research by UNICEF (2007) that placed children and young people in England, Scotland, Northern Ireland and Wales bottom out of 21 developed countries on a range of well-being metrics. This followed a report on youth activity by the Institute for Public Policy Research (IPPR, 2006), which had led many media outlets to report that young people in the UK were 'amongst the worst in Europe' (Guldberg, 2009). This was attributed in part to their poorer social skills, with a key subsequent recommendation being the implementation of 'pedagogic techniques that improve personal and social skills development and behaviour management' (Institute for Public Policy Research, 2006: xiii), providing clear evidence of the youth in crisis model as a driver of SEL. In the wake of riots that took place across several towns and cities in 2011, in which around a quarter of the participants were under the age of 17, this morphed somewhat into concern over the disenfranchising effects of modern British society on children and young people.

In the United States, the youth in crisis model has traditionally focused on violence and substance abuse (Lerner, 1995), with its roots traceable to concerns that emerged initially in the 1970s and 1980s (thus fuelling the fire of the self-esteem movement – see above) and that have been ubiquitous ever since. As with the UK, the youth in crisis discourse has been a key driver of educational policy. So, for example, it paved the way for the Department for Education's Drug-Free Schools and Communities program, which had a budget of more than $660 million by the early 1990s (Gorman, 1998). Similarly, school shootings and other tragic events involving interpersonal violence in the mid-to-late 1990s gripped the attention of policy-makers and led to an increased emphasis on mental health issues in schools, including crisis prevention and intervention, risk assessment and prediction of violence in students (Merrell and Gueldner, 2010).

Evidence for hope rather than despair

Highlighting the youth in crisis model as a key driver of SEL is *not* intended to demean the importance of the variety of issues noted through the discourse. Clearly, things like interpersonal violence and mental health difficulties are important issues that warrant attention and intervention. However, there is a clear need for a critical analysis of the prevalent negative depiction of modern childhood and youth. First, the model is not new or unique to the current generation. It simply takes different forms at different periods in recent history that reflect anxieties that are prevalent at the time. There is evidence stretching back to at least the 1930s of widespread concerns about 'the telltale signs of maladjusted youth' (see, for example, Havighurst, 1974: 6). Indeed, it could be argued that every generation has had its own 'child panic' (Guldberg, 2009).

Second, if we pause to examine the evidence base, it becomes clear that the trend toward increasingly negative outcomes in children and young people that is central to the current youth in crisis model is not always borne out. Take, for example, the Youth Risk Behaviour Surveillance report (CDCP, 2010) which monitors priority health-risk behaviours in the United States. The most recent iteration of this survey of over 16,000 young people aged 10–24 indicated significant *decreases* in the proportion who reported engaging in behaviours that contribute to violence (e.g. weapon carrying, fighting, depression and suicidal ideation) and major types of substance abuse (e.g. smoking, alcohol use) during the period 1991–2009 (CDCP, 2010).

Similarly, in contrast to the aforementioned IPPR and UNICEF reports, large-scale research involving around 10,000 respondents conducted by the Children's Society (2012) has suggested that, on average, children and young people in the UK actually experience positive well-being. Their mean score on an overall well-being measure is about 14–16 out of 20, which is directly comparable to surveys of well-being in adults. Furthermore, when questioned on their happiness with ten aspects of life including family, health, their home, friends, time use and school, they score at or above an average of 7 out of 10 on all but one aspect (the future – which is perhaps understandable given the current economic situation). These positive trends garner much less media attention because of their reduced news values. Of course, they may well be attributable in part to the increased emphasis on SEL in recent years.

 Points for Reflection

- What broad purpose(s) does the youth in crisis model serve?

Risk, protection and resilience

The field of SEL also draws significantly upon the conceptual framework of risk, protection and resilience that has been extremely influential in contemporary developmental psychology. This is evident in the academic literature, policy documentation and practitioner texts. Risk factors are those which are associated with an increased likelihood of problematic outcomes (such as poor academic achievement, mental health problems or involvement in crime), with protective factors conferring the opposite effect (Reicher, 2010). The concept of resilience emerged from work on risk and protection. It describes the process of successful adaptation despite exposure to adversity. Resilience research therefore seeks to determine what is 'different' about children who achieve successful outcomes even though they experience significant risk factors in their daily lives (Poulou, 2007). Resilience factors are often described in terms of internal (e.g. a strong sense of self-efficacy) and external (e.g. positive relationships with teachers) 'assets'.

What is the relationship between this framework and SEL? Resilience is the key here. Like resilience, SEL focuses on the notion of strengths and competence. Furthermore, the core aims, objectives and context of SEL align closely with several of the key 'adaptive systems' that play a central role in fostering resilience, including the attachment system (e.g. relationships with caregivers), the self-regulation system (e.g. management of emotions), the school system (e.g. teaching) and the peer system (e.g. development and maintenance of friendships) (Masten and Obradovic, 2006). Similarly, Harvey and Delfabbro's (2004) review of the characteristics of resilient children identified several that are intended primary outcomes of SEL, including good empathy and problem-solving skills. SEL in part draws its rationale from the concept of resilience, and the process of explicit SEL instruction can therefore be seen as a direct attempt to provide all children with resilience-enhancing experiences. Indeed, the 'essential components' of the experiences that have been identified through research on resilience align closely with fundamental elements of SEL – such as the importance of caring relationships and opportunities to contribute to other people (Reicher, 2010).

However, there are also some caveats in the 'SEL as resilience-enhancing' analogy. The first is conceptual. It can be argued that there is a discord between the concept of resilience, which by definition can only be considered an attribute among children *exposed to risk* (that is, there must be something adverse against which children can demonstrate resilience), and the universalist model of SEL, which proposes that *all* children need explicit instruction to enhance core social and emotional competencies. In a sense this returns us to the issue noted in the previous chapter, which is that SEL involves a fundamental 'trade-off', whereby much of the effort expended is on children who are unlikely to develop difficulties anyway, in the hope that problems can be prevented in a minority whose exposure to adversity places them at significant risk.

A second limitation is that the analogy of SEL as resilience-enhancing does not necessarily reflect the complex processes involved in the operation of resilient characteristics and behaviour on outcomes. The characteristics noted above may have direct influences, or they may play a role as moderators or mediators of outcomes (e.g. by influencing the relationship between a given risk or stressor and an outcome) (Reicher, 2010). Furthermore, Masten and Obradovic (2006) note that the resilience demonstrated by individuals may vary as a function of context, time, stressor and adaptive domain.

This is at odds with the 'inoculation metaphor' underpinning SEL. By way of an example, consider the research introduced in the previous chapter which suggested that EI moderates the relationship between chronic stressors and mental health outcomes in adolescents (Davis and Humphrey, 2012b). There was clear evidence of the type of variation noted by Masten and Obradovic (2006) in this study. For example, the analyses suggested that EI moderated the effects of some stressors (e.g. family dysfunction, socio-economic adversity) but not others (e.g. negative life events). There was further variation according to the both the type of EI and the outcome in question, with trait EI operating on internalising but not externalising symptoms, and the reverse being true for ability EI (note: the distinction between trait and ability EI will be addressed in Chapter 5). Finally, in certain risk contexts (specifically, where young people were exposed to extremely high socio-economic adversity), higher-ability EI was actually associated with *greater* internalising problems relative to those with lower-ability EI. Such evidence suggests that the notion of SEL competencies as being universally adaptive resilience characteristics is an oversimplification.

The field of school-based prevention

As noted in the previous chapter, at a conceptual level SEL sits within the broader field of prevention. This is also the case historically, where many prototypical SEL programmes grew from attempts to prevent interpersonal violence, mental health problems and substance abuse. For example, the Second Step programme, featured in the next chapter, was developed by the Committee for Children in Seattle as a means of preventing violence and abuse following their earlier, more 'reactive' work in this area (hence the title of the programme). Like SEL, the field of prevention has a history dating back for thousands of years, although the most progress and development – particularly in relation to mental health – has inarguably been in the twentieth century. This period saw the development of efforts to prevent physical ill health, psychological problems and the social conditions that disturb well-being (e.g. poverty) (Hage and Romano, 2010). Prevention focused around and practised through schools emerged during this time, with the first examples relating to school-based mental health programmes appearing from the 1920s, although the most rapid expansion began much later in the 1980s (Durlak, 1995). Schools are seen as ideal settings for prevention activity. As Greenberg (2010) states, 'By virtue of their central role in lives of children and families and their broad reach, schools are the primary setting in which many initial concerns arise and can be effectively remediated' (p. 28).

What influence has the field of prevention had on SEL? An obvious place to start is the reach component of the taxonomy introduced in Chapter 1 – that of universal, targeted and indicated intervention. This is drawn directly from the definitions of *primary* (for everyone – stopping a problem before it happens), *secondary* (for those at risk of developing a problem) and *tertiary* (for those showing signs or already beginning to experience difficulties) prevention outlined in Caplan's (1964) seminal *Principles of Prevention Psychiatry*.

A further aspect of the relationship between the field of prevention and SEL is the focus on promotion. As we saw in the previous chapter, prevention and promotion are essentially two sides of the same coin, but what is important about the notion of promotion embodied in SEL is that it reflects a movement away from a 'sickness' model to a humanistic approach that emphasises positive development and human potential (Hage and Romano, 2010). This moves SEL beyond the basic inoculation metaphor introduced earlier, because it becomes less about simply preventing a negative outcome (which, as we have seen in this chapter and elsewhere, is a flawed model) and more about facilitating growth and self-actualisation. In this sense, the promotional focus of SEL is a direct counter to the claims of critics such as Ecclestone and Hayes (2008) that it is based on a diminished view of human potential.

The political and financial drivers of SEL

Having explored some of the influences on the development of SEL, our journey now takes us to the forces that drive it in the current educational milieu. Although presented separately, they are necessarily interrelated.

The politics of SEL

Let us first consider the political drivers of SEL. England provides a useful case study. Here, SEL grew in popularity and appeal during the reign of the Labour party (which lasted from 1997 to 2010) as part of a much broader political agenda relating to well-being. This agenda developed from internal forces such as child poverty, anti-social behaviour and the need to develop 'employability' in young people (Watson et al., 2012), in addition to the external factors noted earlier in this chapter (e.g. UNICEF, 2007). Broad-brush policies like *Every Child Matters* (Department for Education and Skills, 2003) and *The Children's Plan* (Department for Children, Schools and Families, 2007) were supplemented with numerous national strategies/initiatives such as the SEAL programme as a means of demonstrating the value attributed to social and emotional well-being by the government and also their responsibility for and commitment to enhancing it among the nation's children and young people. However, this period of government also saw the introduction of the 'standards agenda' (Ainscow et al., 2006), in which school league tables, targets and inspections drove schools to narrowly focus their efforts on academic attainment. Concerns about the marginalising effects of the standards agenda were particularly strong for the more vulnerable children in schools: 'The inexorable pressure of the curriculum, examinations/ SATs requirements and league tables demand that mainstream teachers drive forward in a way that may not be conducive to good inclusive practice' (HOCESC, 2006: 66).

England has not been alone in experiencing contradictions and discord in the political machinations relating to SEL. A similar picture emerged in the United States, where the No Child Left Behind Act of 2001 passed into law a variety of mandates that focused on SEL and related areas (e.g. mental health). These included grants to establish or expand counselling services in schools, closer integration between schools and community mental health service providers, and the promotion of school readiness through SEL interventions in early childhood (Daly et al., 2006). However, the primary focus of NCLB was similar to the standards agenda in England – standards and accountability took precedence, with frequent assessment the order of the day (Merrell and Gueldner, 2010). Kress et al. (2004) suggest that this shift in schools' accountability structures was seen as incompatible with the continuation of SEL and other prevention-related initiatives.

What are we to make of this 'dissonance'? It is certainly difficult to reconcile these divergent policy objectives. They may simply reflect a lack of true conviction on the part of governments in relation to the value attributed to the universal promotion of SEL when compared to the economically driven 'need' to focus on academic attainment as the most important outcome of schooling (Kress et al., 2004). That is, governments are prepared to acknowledge the significance of SEL, but when 'push comes to shove' they take comfort in focusing their major policies on traditional, rationalist models embodied in academic outcomes. This has clear and consistent effects 'at the chalkface', where school staff consistently cite the need to prioritise academic attainment as a barrier to their continued investment in SEL (see Chapter 6). Of course, what this discord neglects is the hypothesis that promoting SEL will yield subsequent academic benefits for students. Perhaps educators themselves remain sceptical about this notion? Recent evidence to support the SEL-attainment link (e.g. Durlak et al., 2011) may go some way to convincing them if this is indeed the case.

Points for Reflection

- What might underpin the educational 'policy paradox', wherein SEL appears to be at once both promoted and stifled by the machinations of politicians?

The economics of SEL

Sitting alongside the rather uncertain political drivers of SEL there are also financial considerations that warrant attention. Chief among these is the economic argument for SEL. The annual cost of mental health disorders among young people in the United States is estimated to be around $247 billion (O'Connell et al., 2009). In the United Kingdom, the annual cost *per child* for mental health services to address complex difficulties is £50,000 (Clark et al., 2005). The growth that could be associated with improved academic attainment of the magnitude reported by Durlak et al. (2011) is also an important consideration, as the economics literature suggests that this could produce around a 5 per cent increase in lifetime earnings (Duncan and Magnuson, 2007). At an intuitive level then, if we accept that the outcomes of universal programmes include reduced mental health difficulties and increased academic attainment, then SEL is one of the most sound economic investments that could be made. However, the evidence base pertaining to the benefits and costs of SEL is still in its infancy (Hummel et al., 2009; McCabe, 2008; O'Connell et al., 2009), making it difficult to draw sound conclusions (see Chapter 7).

 Further Reading

Dixon, T. (2012) 'Educating the emotions from Gradgrind to Goleman', *Research Papers in Education*, 27: 481–95.
Guldberg, H. (2009). *Reclaiming Childhood: Freedom and Play in an Age of Fear*. London: Routledge.

4

SEL around the world

Overview

In this chapter we will explore the current status of SEL in educational policy and practice across the world. The available space does not permit a completely comprehensive analysis as there are far too many countries dabbling with SEL for this to be feasible. Instead, I present a range of contrasting exemplar case studies, namely the USA, England, Northern Ireland, Australia, Sweden, and Singapore. The chapter concludes with an analysis of the convergences and divergences in SEL policy and practice across these different countries.

Key Points

- SEL is a dominant force in education systems around the world.
- The shape it has taken in different countries is influenced by a variety of cultural, political and social factors.
- There is considerable 'cross fertilisation' of SEL, with a number of nations experimenting with cultural adaptations of existing programmes in addition to the development of their own bespoke interventions.
- Some key areas of divergence are evident in the influence of policy, the role played by evidence and the level of prescriptiveness evident in approaches to SEL in different countries.

The United States

It seems sensible to begin our international journey in the United States (US) since they have inarguably been the trailblazers in the development and implementation of SEL in schools. As noted earlier, the major focus on this area in the American education system was primarily influenced by fears of a growing culture of school violence, substance abuse and other 'risk' behaviours. However, as the movement has grown there has been a shift in focus, such that there is an increased emphasis on the promotional aspects of SEL, particularly in relation to academic achievement. This is due in part to the growth of the evidence base (e.g. Durlak et al., 2011), but is also a response to the increased focus on academic standards and accountability in educational reform in the US in the last decade (see Chapter 3) (Merrell and Gueldner, 2010).

The US is also an interesting case study because, unlike some other countries (e.g. England, Northern Ireland), there has never been a 'national' SEL programme or initiative. Indeed, because of the 10th Amendment, the majority of educational policy is decided at state level (or, indeed, at district level), with the exception of major education acts. An example of this is the Elementary and Secondary Education Act (also known as the 'No Child Left Behind Act'), which has recently been reauthorised and updated to include the development of social and emotional competencies as part of Title IV – 'Successful, Safe and Healthy Students'. As a result, the US contains the greatest diversity of SEL interventions in the world (as noted previously, CASEL reported there to be in excess of 240 nearly a decade ago) (CASEL, 2003).

As noted in Chapter 1, in most US states SEL is integrated into mandated K-12 learning standards, with one (Illinois) having explicit, free-standing SEL goals and benchmarks (Dusenbury et al., 2011). Schools work towards these standards through explicit SEL instruction. In Illinois, which has led the way in integrating SEL into education, around 60 per cent of schools report implementing a particular SEL curriculum, with the same proportions also engaging in staff professional development for SEL and making changes to their school policies and procedures as part of their implementation efforts in this area (Institute of Government and Public Affairs, 2011).

Any attempt to provide detailed coverage of the massive number of SEL interventions that are available to schools in the US would be an exercise in futility. Instead, I provide some exemplar case studies, all of which are in use in a number of US states, and many of which have also been adopted internationally (see later sections of this chapter).

Promoting Alternative Thinking Strategies

The PATHS programme was developed by Carol Kusche and Mark Greenberg and was initially used as a preventive intervention for deaf children (Greenberg and Kusche, 1993). Its utility with children in special (Kam et al., 2004) and mainstream education (Greenberg et al., 1995) has since been explored. PATHS is built around the 'Affective-Behavioural-Cognitive-Dynamic' (ABCD) model of development, which focuses on the developmental integration of affect, emotion language, behaviour and cognitive understanding to promote social and emotional competence (Greenberg and Kusche, 1993).

The curriculum comprises a series of lessons across five volumes and one readiness unit that focus upon developing children's self-control, emotional awareness and interpersonal problem-solving. It is designed to be delivered by class teachers for approximately one hour per week throughout the school year with children aged 4–11. The lessons cover topics including identifying and labelling feelings, expressing feelings, assessing the intensity of feelings, managing feelings, understanding the difference between feelings and behaviours, delaying gratification, controlling impulses, reducing stress, self-talk, reading and interpreting social cues, understanding others' perspectives, using steps for problem-solving and decision-making, self-awareness, non-verbal communication skills and verbal communication skills (CSVP, 2006). PATHS reflects an 'eco-behavioral systems orientation' (Greenberg et al., 2004), an approach which recognises that interventions that focus on the child or the environment alone are not as effective as those that consider both in tandem. Thus the programme emphasises skill building, the development of adaptive relationships (teacher–child and child–child), the teacher's approach to interaction, and complete integration of the intervention at classroom and school levels (CSVP, 2006).

PATHS is, in many ways, the archetypal American SEL programme. Its emphasis is on the development of social and emotional skills through the teaching of an explicit curriculum. This curriculum is very tightly sequenced, and the lessons themselves are scripted for teachers. Hence, there is a great deal of emphasis on fidelity in implementation. In our taxonomy of SEL programmes introduced in Chapter 1, PATHS is very much a 'top-down' rather than a 'bottom-up' intervention. Although some elements of the programme link to work with parents and on the school ethos/environment, it is nonetheless primarily a single-component approach with an emphasis on universal provision.

Caring School Community

The Caring School Community (CSC) programme began life as the Child Development Project (CDP) in the early 1980s. It provides an interesting contrast to PATHS (above) inasmuch as its focus is primarily on the improving the school environment as opposed to the teaching of a social and emotional curriculum. It is described by its founders as an 'ecological approach to intervention' (Battistich et al., 2000: 76). CSC aims to build a strong sense of community within the school, based around four principles (Lewis et al., 2003):

1. Building secure, supportive relationships within and between children, school staff and parents.
2. Encouraging children to collaborate and cooperate with others.
3. Allowing students to exercise influence and autonomy.
4. Discussion and reflection on key values and ideals.

CSC is based upon a theoretical framework that incorporates influences from work on socialisation, attachment theory, learning and motivation, and pro-social development, the key tenets of which are that participating in a caring school community will (a) facilitate students' academic, social and moral development, and (b) meet their basic psychological needs, such as feelings of autonomy and belonging (Battistich et al., 1999; Battistich et al., 2000).

The content of CSC has evolved over time. The main departure from the original programme (CDP) is that the latter originally contained a distinct academic component involving literature-based reading instruction (Solomon et al., 2000) which is now offered as a separate, optional enhancement to the programme. In its current form, there are four key components emphasised in the guidance materials. The first of these, class meetings, give teachers and students a forum for discussing issues and identifying and solving problems collaboratively, and are also used as a means for increasing student autonomy (through, for example, setting norms and rules). The second component involves the implementation of a cross-age 'buddy' system in which younger and older classes of children are paired for a variety of academic and non-academic activities with the aim of building relationships and trust. The third component, 'homeside activities', constitutes the parental involvement element of CSC, and consists of a series of activities that begin in the classroom, and are subsequently extended to the home environment before students report back, with the aim of creating a 'cycle of learning' and promoting interpersonal understanding. The final element of the programme involves whole-school activities designed to promote a sense of community and foster links between children, their parents and school staff (Institute of Education Sciences, 2007).

In our taxonomy of SEL interventions, CSC is, like PATHS, a universal intervention with a fairly prescriptive (e.g. top-down) implementation rubric. However, it differs from PATHS in that it is multi-component (incorporating distinct strands that focus on school ethos/environment and parents).

Second Step

Second Step was developed by the Committee for Children (CfC) in Seattle, who began work as a non-profit organisation working to end child sexual abuse in the late 1970s. They originally developed a curriculum and adult training programme called 'Talking About Touching', which represented the 'first step' in stopping violence and abuse. In the mid-1980s CfC began to engage in more preventive (as opposed to reactive) work, and hence developed Second Step. The original version of the programme was informed by the research of figures such as Albert Bandura and Norma Feshbach. The intervention itself is classroom-based and designed to promote school success and prevent problem behaviour among children and young people aged 4–14 by improving their social and emotional skills (Committee for Children, 2011). In many ways it is very similar to the PATHS programme, being a universal intervention, primarily curriculum-based, developmentally sequenced and with a strong emphasis on fidelity of implementation. The programme is based upon a model of risk and protective factors for problem behaviours. The most recent update of Second Step (released in 2011) emphasises the development of key executive functions or 'skills for learning' – self-regulation, self-management, listening, focusing and paying attention. These foundations are supplemented with instruction designed to develop empathy, emotion management and problem-solving (Committee for Children, 2011).

Second Step consists of a series of lessons differentiated according to year group that focus upon empathy and communication, bullying prevention, emotion management, substance abuse prevention and goal setting. Lessons consist of structured activities led by an adult facilitator (e.g. teacher) that include group discussion, individual, partner and group activities, interactive exercises, games and skills practice (McMahon et al., 2000). Many lessons are supported by multimedia input (e.g. informational video clips, dramatic vignettes). There are also online resources, and indeed training for teachers is now delivered online.

 Points for Reflection

- Why has the 'top-down', manualised approach to SEL been so dominant in the US?

England

SEL in England is best embodied by the Social and Emotional Aspects of Learning (SEAL) programme. SEAL was a National Strategy launched in the primary school sector in 2005 (Department for Education and Skills, 2005b) and in the secondary school sector in 2007 (Department for Education and Skills, 2007a). By the time that the new coalition government took power in 2010, SEAL was estimated to be in use in 90 per cent of primary schools and 70 per cent of secondary schools (Humphrey et al., 2010). Although the new government has 'officially' discontinued SEAL (BBC, 2011), the materials developed are still in use in a great number of schools across the country.

SEAL emerged from the confluence of a number of related influences and factors. At the policy level, the previous government was under pressure to redress the technicism in the English education system embodied by the 'standards agenda' (e.g. narrowly focused league tables, targets and inspection regimes) (Ainscow et al., 2006). In the early part of the last decade, they began to develop more holistic policy directives with a focus on promoting well-being (e.g. *Every Child Matters* – Department for Education and Skills, 2003). Around the same time, Weare and Gray published an influential review, funded by the Department for Education and Skills, entitled *What Works in Promoting Children's Emotional and Social Competence and Wellbeing?* (Weare and Gray, 2003). One of the key recommendations of their report was the prioritisation, development and implementation of a national, school-based programme to promote social and emotional skills in pupils and staff. Finally, as seen in Chapter 3, Daniel Goleman's (1996) bestseller had brought the concept of EI (and its claimed importance in education, the workplace and life in general) into the public consciousness. These factors ultimately led to the Department for Education and Skills commissioning a new National

Strategy as part of the Behaviour and Attendance pilot, and the SEAL programme was born.

SEAL is described as 'a comprehensive approach to promoting the social and emotional skills that underpin effective learning, positive behaviour, regular attendance, staff effectiveness and the emotional health and wellbeing of all who learn and work in schools' (Department for Children, Schools and Families, 2007: 4). The influence of Goleman (1996) is reflected in the core taxonomy of skills that the programme is designed to promote – namely self-awareness, self-regulation, motivation, empathy and social skills. SEAL's constituent components are: (a) the use of a whole-school approach to create a positive school climate and ethos; (b) direct teaching of social and emotional skills in whole-class contexts; (c) the use of teaching and learning approaches that support the learning of such skills; and (d) continuing professional development for school staff (Department for Children, Schools and Families, 2007). In both the primary and secondary versions of SEAL, implementation support materials are presented thematically. For example, in primary SEAL, schools begin the new academic year by working through the 'New Beginnings' theme in which 'children explore feelings of happiness and excitement, sadness, anxiety and fearfulness, while learning (and putting into practice) shared models for "calming down" and "problem-solving" (Department for Education and Skills, 2006: 1). Implementation of this and other SEAL themes follows the 'waves of intervention' model promoted by the National Strategies, which is essentially akin to the 'reach' component of the SEL taxonomy introduced in Chapter 1 (e.g. universal/targeted/indicated).

SEAL implementation in schools was supported by a number of guidance documents and materials pertaining to its different components (e.g. 'family SEAL', 'SEAL small group work') and versions (e.g. 'primary SEAL', 'secondary SEAL'), and training offered in LAs by Behaviour and Attendance consultants and other professionals working in Children's Services. As a programme, it provides an interesting contrast to the SEL interventions developed in the US in that it is envisaged as a loose enabling framework for school improvement (Weare, 2010) rather than a structured 'package' to be applied in schools. Schools (particularly in secondary SEAL) are actively encouraged to explore different approaches to implementation that support identified school improvement priorities rather than following a single model. This philosophy was reflected in the absence of materials for some components. For example, in the primary SEAL small group work guidance, materials were only available for four of the seven themed interventions, with school staff encouraged to develop their own (Department for Education and Skills, 2006). In the guidance produced for secondary schools, a variety of contrasting implementation case studies were included (Department for Children Schools and Families, 2007). In this sense, SEAL represents the diametric opposite of the top-down, manualised SEL interventions that have been popular in the US (see above).

Although the SEAL programme has been very much the dominant approach to SEL taken in English schools, it is by no means the only intervention that schools have been implementing. Some LAs and schools have opted to adopt existing SEL approaches to supplement or as an alternative to SEAL. For example, the PATHS programme was adopted in Winchester from 2002 (Curtis and Norgate, 2007), and has recently been rolled out in schools across Birmingham as part of the Brighter Futures strategy (Little and Hopkins, 2010). Other initiatives related to SEL that have been used in English schools include the UK Resilience Programme (Penn Resilience Programme) (Challen et al., 2011), and the Targeted Mental Health in Schools programme (Wolpert et al., 2011) (note that, despite its name, the TaMHS programme incorporated elements of both universal and targeted provision).

Northern Ireland

The emotional well-being of pupils has been identified as a policy priority by government ministers in Northern Ireland, at least in part because of the country's social and political history (e.g. 'The Troubles') (Connolly et al., 2011; Muldoon, 2004; O'Reilly and Stevenson, 2003). Reflecting this, the recently revised Northern Ireland Curriculum includes a statutory Personal Development and Mutual Understanding (PDMU) strand (Partnership Management Board, 2007). PDMU is used in the primary phase of education in Northern Ireland. The post-primary school curriculum contains a Learning for Life and Work (LLW) strand that contains SEL material in the Personal Development section.

PDMU is similar in many ways to the SEAL programme in England (although SEAL was never statutory in English schools). Like SEAL, PDMU provides a loose framework, intended to be 'a starting point for reflection and whole-school review' (Partnership Management Board, 2007: 1) rather than a prescriptive, step-by-step SEL curriculum. Support materials are also presented thematically – for example, 'Feelings and Emotions', 'Learning to Learn' – with sample learning activities and links to suggested resources (Department for Education in Northern Ireland, 2007). The focus of PDMU also has a similar feel to SEAL – for example, developing pupils' self-awareness, self-management and working with others – although perhaps because of social and political factors mentioned above, the programme more explicitly deals with community issues (e.g. 'the need for mutual understanding and respect in the community and in the wider world') (Partnership Management Board, 2007: 5).

Alongside PDMU, in 2007 the Department for Education in Northern Ireland (DENI) began to develop the Pupils' Emotional Health and Wellbeing programme (PEHW). PEHW is intended to act as a central hub through which the services that have an impact on pupils' emotional health may be integrated (Connolly et al., 2011). Although still in development at the time of writing, the project has established five working groups focusing on self-assessment for schools, the training and support needs of school staff, good practice identification and dissemination, mapping available resources and response to critical incidents (e.g. suicide). At present, a brief set of materials has been made available to schools that include posters, leaflets, homework diary inserts and resource links organised around ten topics of concern to children and young people (e.g. 'Feelings', 'Keeping Safe'). These materials represent a very 'light touch' approach that is based around information-giving, awareness-raising and signposting.

A recent scoping survey of current practice relating to SEL in Northern Ireland (Connolly et al., 2011) gives an indication that schools there are also making use of existing interventions, including the SEAL programme from England (Department for Education and Skills, 2007a) and MindMatters from Australia (Wyn et al., 2000). Additionally, a number of the major evidence-based SEL interventions from the US, including the PATHS curriculum (Greenberg et al., 2004) and the Incredible Years training series (McGilloway et al., 2010), have also been adopted by some schools.

Australia

SEL provision in Australia is organised predominantly around national programmes for the different phases of education. Beyond this, there are also some different regional initiatives. The nature of the two main programmes that have been launched nationally is such that there is a great diversity of specific interventions being implemented on the ground (see below).

'KidsMatter' represents the Australian government's main SEL-related initiative for primary schools (Australian Government

Department of Health and Ageing, 2009). There are three different versions, designed to cover early childhood (e.g. pre-school and day-care), primary schools, and a parent-focused package designed to ease the transition from the former to the latter. KidsMatter is comprised of four components, which in combination mirror the graduated model of support seen in SEL initiatives in many other countries (e.g. SEAL in England). The first component, 'A Positive School Community', focuses on developing the school ethos and environment such that it promotes mental health, respectful relationships and a sense of belonging among students and staff. The second component, 'Social and Emotional Learning for Students', aims to provide an effective SEL curriculum for all children and allow them opportunities to practise and transfer their skills. The third component, 'Working with Parents and Carers', promotes collaboration between schools and parents/carers, provides support for parents in relation to their children's mental health and helps to develop parent and carer support networks. Finally, the 'Helping Children Experiencing Mental Health Difficulties' component aims to expand schools' understanding of mental health difficulties, improve help-seeking and develop appropriate responses (e.g. interventions). Materials and resources (e.g. guidance documents, information sheets) are provided to support each of these strands, in addition to professional development/training opportunities for school staff (Slee et al., 2009).

KidsMatter provides an interesting case study in relation to our taxonomy of SEL interventions introduced in Chapter 1. Like many other initiatives covered in this chapter, it provides a graduated model of support from the universal (components 1–3) to the targeted/indicated (component 4). Given its different components, it is a multi-component intervention. However, in terms of the degree of prescriptiveness evident, it is very much in the middle, providing a balance between flexibility and rigidity. So, for each of the different components, all schools are provided with the same basic materials and resources which they are expected to supplement by implementing existing programmes. The KidsMatter resource (http://www.kidsmatter.edu.au) provides schools with a guide to over 70 available interventions, with information covering the areas of focus, evidence base, theoretical framework, structure and other factors to enable them to make informed choices that suit their local context and needs. So, for example, a KidsMatter school might choose to implement Steps to Respect (Frey et al., 2005) to fulfil the positive school community component, the Social Decision Making/Social Problem Solving programme (Elias et al., 1986) as their social and emotional learning curriculum, the Triple P programme (Sanders et al., 2002) to support the parental strand and the FRIENDS for Life intervention (Stallard et al., 2005) as part of their package of targeted support for children experiencing difficulties.

'Mindmatters' is the national initiative for secondary education in Australia, and is estimated to be in use in around 66 per cent of all secondary schools (Australian Council for Educational Research, 2010). In contrast to provision in other parts of the world (where the primary sector has led the way in SEL) it was actually launched a decade *prior* to KidsMatter. It comprises a resource kit for schools with eight booklets that support activity in a number of areas (for example, there is a seven-session taught curriculum designed to help students understand mental illness), a series of tiered professional development activities, and extensive online and multimedia support. As with KidsMatter, it is presented as a framework for the integration of existing initiatives and interventions at the universal, targeted and indicated levels of provision (Wyn et al., 2000). MindMatters differs from KidsMatter somewhat in that it does not have an 'explicit' component that is specifically focused on developing SEL, but nonetheless one of its key aims is to 'develop the social and emotional skills required to meet life's challenges' (http://www.mindmatters.edu.au).

 Points for Reflection

- What difficulties might the more flexible approaches to SEL provision create in terms of conducting rigorous evaluations?

Sweden

SEL in the Swedish education system began to develop in the early-to-mid 1990s. During that time, the government released a national curriculum plan, which promoted a holistic view of the role of schooling, incorporating a greater emphasis on schools' pastoral functions than had previously been present (Dahlin, 2008). The present version of this national curriculum contains several objectives that relate directly or indirectly to SEL, including the promotion of respect and mutual support among students, and the development of empathy and feelings of community and responsibility in relation to school (National Agency for Education, 2006). So, while there has never been a national SEL policy in Sweden (compared to, for example, the SEAL initiative in England), certain core values in the national curriculum reflect perceptions of the importance of this area. However, the Swedish National Agency for Education's ('Skolverket') current position is that SEL should *not* be taught explicitly as a stand-alone curriculum, but rather should be infused into regular lessons within the academic curriculum (Kimber, 2011a). This has not stopped the development of bespoke interventions like the Social and Emotional Training (SET) programme, a universal SEL curriculum designed to be taught throughout the primary and secondary phases of education (Kimber, 2011b). The SET programme focuses on the same five SEL competencies as the SEAL initiative in England – that is, self-awareness, self-regulation, empathy, motivation and social skills (Kimber et al., 2008), and was inspired by the aforementioned PATHS programme (Kimber, 2011b). Sweden has also been active in importing existing SEL programmes from elsewhere, including the aforementioned Second Step (Dahlin, 2008), although this has slowed recently in response to the National Agency for Education's directive, noted above.

Singapore

The development of SEL in the island city-state of Singapore found its impetus from a need to rebalance a curriculum that, while producing excellent academic results (e.g. in the Programme for International Student Assessment), was perhaps felt to be lacking in input that would help students to become resilient and resourceful (Kom, 2011). Just over a decade ago, Singapore's Ministry of Education produced a landmark document entitled *Desired Outcomes of Education* (Ministry of Education, 2001), which outlined a vision for the preferred attributes of learners at the end of different stages of education. Many of these related directly to SEL, for example 'be able to co-operate, share, and care for others' (primary), 'have moral integrity', 'be able to work in teams and show empathy for others' (both secondary) and 'be resilient in the face of adversity' (post-secondary). From around 2004, work began to develop an SEL framework through a systematic progression process that included planning (including studies of 'best practice' in SEL from other education systems), development (including building a set of SEL standards and benchmarks), implementation (including rolling out the framework in schools) and review (including evaluation) (Kom, 2011).

The SEL Framework that emerged from this work centred around an implementation plan that included four key components – prototyping, training, curriculum and evaluation. *Prototyping* is essentially an action research model, in which schools are encouraged to focus on specific outcomes, develop different approaches to meeting them (for example, experimenting with different strategies, including existing programmes) (Kom, 2011) and testing these systematically. This very flexible approach was designed specifically to facilitate ownership and sustainability, much like the SEAL programme in England. *Training* was put in place to ensure that both existing and trainee teachers were able to implement such approaches in schools. A set of curriculum resources was developed to facilitate the infusion of SEL into the *curriculum*. Finally, an *evaluation* framework (with accompanying tools) was developed in order to allow schools to assess their own progress (Kom, 2011).

Convergences and divergences in SEL across the world – an analysis

The case studies of SEL in different countries presented above hopefully demonstrate just how central it has become in education systems across the world in recent years. As noted, space does not allow a completely comprehensive look, but if it did, strong evidence of SEL in other countries including Wales, Scotland, Canada, the Netherlands, Spain, Germany, Portugal, Finland and elsewhere could also have been presented (Marcelino Botín Foundation, 2011; Watson et al., 2012). In examining policy and practice in these countries, there are some key themes that begin to emerge, to which we now turn our attention.

A first key theme is the role played by government policy, and here we find some stark contrasts. In the US, educational policy is largely decentralised, meaning that states and school districts have much more freedom in terms of which educational innovations they choose to adopt. This creates a 'free market' situation in which programme developers essentially compete with one another to 'build a better mousetrap' (Durlak and DuPre, 2008). The result is a large and diverse set of SEL programmes, with great variation in adoption within and across states and districts. This contrasts sharply with England, where educational policy has largely been centralised (until our recent change of government), allowing national strategies like the SEAL programme to very quickly become orthodoxies. Indeed, as noted earlier, SEAL was being implemented in most primary and secondary schools across the country just five years after it was initially piloted in the primary sector.

The second key theme is the role played by evidence. In the US, with its free market approach to SEL, evidence has to be an important consideration because it becomes a selling point for programme developers. Indeed, funding streams for schools in this area often dictate that only 'proven' programmes can be considered. In countries like England, because centralisation means that there is essentially no 'competition', evidence becomes a secondary consideration. Given this, it is perhaps unsurprising that both the primary and secondary versions of the SEAL programme were launched nationally before their pilot evaluations were reported. Somewhere between these two contrasting situations sits Australia, which has a largely centralised SEL framework (e.g. KidsMatter), but one that has been subjected to evaluation prior to being brought to scale (indeed, the announcement of funding to support an expansion of the initiative was published in the foreword of Slee et al.'s (2009) pilot evaluation report), and one that still enabled choice (and therefore competition between programme developers) at each level of implementation.

The overview of SEL policy and provision in different countries also highlights the contrast between top-down and bottom-up approaches to SEL. In the United States, there has been a strong tradition of prescriptive, manualised approaches and an emphasis on fidelity of implementation. This contrasts with the approach taken in many European countries, Australia and Singapore, where there is less rigidity and more flexibility. Weare and Nind (2011) attribute this difference to the influence of agencies such as the European Commission and the World Health Organisation, whose fundamental principles of empowerment, autonomy, democracy, local adaptability and ownership have generated a more flexible, need-responsive approach. However, there is also an acknowledgement that such approaches may be more difficult to evaluate using traditional methods (e.g. randomised controlled trials): 'the evidence generated by [the flexible approaches] has been weak in terms of hard outcomes' (Weare and Nind, 2011: 62).

A related issue is the contrast between single- and multi-component approaches to SEL that are adopted in different parts of the world. In the United States there has arguably been a trend towards single-component approaches, with the delivery of a taught curriculum the primary mode through which SEL is developed in children and young people. (Of course, there are some clear exceptions to this, including the aforementioned Caring School Community programme.) As noted in Chapter 2, this trend contrasts somewhat with the SEL logic model, which emphasises both the school ethos/environment *and* the explicit teaching of social and emotional skills as the best means to maximise student outcomes. In Europe and Australia there are clearer examples of truly whole-school, multi-component approaches, but ironically the evidence base for them is not as well developed (Weare and Nind, 2011).

What SEL actually means, the function it is intended to serve and how it is imparted in schools can also be seen to vary from country to country. It is this area where we can see the influence of the underpinning cultural values and beliefs of each country most clearly. So, for example, the US 'version' of SEL arguably has closer ties to notions of character education and morality than is evident elsewhere. This is perhaps because of the alignment with conservatism and religion noted in the previous chapter, both of which are a part of America's cultural history. In Sweden, SEL has emerged 'organically' as part of a broader, holistic model of education that is in keeping with core Swedish values of democracy, individual freedom and tolerance (Shuayb and O'Donnell, 2008). Finally, the development and form of SEL in Northern Ireland through the PDMU education strand – most notably the emphasis on mutual understanding and respect in the community – is at least in part attributable to aspects of their social and political history.

 Further Reading

Marcelino Botín Foundation (2011) *Social and Emotional Education: An International Analysis*. Santander, Spain: MBF.
Weare, K. and Nind, M. (2011) *Promoting Mental Health of Children and Adolescents Through Schools and School-Based Interventions*. Southampton: University of Southampton.

5

Assessment

Overview

The aim of this chapter is to examine the means by which approaches to SEL may be assessed. Particular attention is given to how we may measure children's social and emotional competence. I discuss a range of issues, including methods of assessment, maximal versus typical behaviour, who provides responses and cultural issues. The chapter continues with a selected anthology of measures, before concluding with consideration of more distal variables that may be monitored as part of a comprehensive evaluation of an SEL intervention.

Key Points

- Assessment, monitoring and evaluation of SEL is vitally important, but is often an afterthought at the level of practice.
- A range of methods of assessment are available. For a variety of reasons, rating scales tend to be the most widely utilised.
- The distinction between typical and maximal behaviour has important implications for what exactly is being assessed, but this has yet to be explored fully with regard to SEL.
- Different informants (e.g. children, their peers, teachers and parents) provide unique perspectives on SEL and hence multi-informant evaluation is to be encouraged.

- With a few notable exceptions, tools used to evaluate SEL have only been validated on Anglo-American populations.
- The CASEL logic model provides useful indicators of the types of distal variables that could be assessed as part of a comprehensive approach to monitoring the impact of SEL. These include mental health, attitudes towards school and outcomes such as academic performance.

The importance of assessment

Assessment, monitoring and evaluation are central components of schooling. They are 'woven into the fabric of school experience' (Merrell and Gueldner, 2010: 123). Educational policy developments in countries across the world in the last two decades have only served to reinforce and strengthen this notion. For example, as has already been noted, both the No Child Left Behind Act (NCLB) in the US and the 'standards agenda' (Ainscow et al., 2006) in England provided test-driven, standards-and-accountability-focused legislation. Put bluntly, schools rise or fall based upon their academic test results. This, of course, is highly controversial, but it is beyond the scope and remit of this text to explore fully.

Given that assessment, monitoring and evaluation in relation to academic standards and competencies are the norm, it is perhaps somewhat surprising that the same cannot be said in relation to SEL. At the practice level, key figures in the field such as the late Kenneth Merrell have suggested that assessment in relation to SEL is often an afterthought (Merrell and Gueldner, 2010). Our experience in evaluating the SEAL programme in England (Humphrey et al., 2008; Humphrey et al., 2010) resonates strongly with this observation. We rarely found schools which routinely assessed, monitored and evaluated their progress in this area in any systematic way. Why might this be the case? Although the pressures to demonstrate academic standards may be an influence, there are undoubtedly other reasons. It is not necessarily because SEL isn't seen as being important – up until recently, for example, part of the school inspection process in England (overseen by the Office for Standards in Education) involved assessment of the extent to which they had appropriate provision in place to enhance pupils' personal development and well-being (Northen, 2012), meaning that it was in schools' interests to provide evidence of the effectiveness of their practice in this regard. As noted earlier in this book, in many US states SEL is integrated into mandated K-12 learning standards, with one (Illinois) having explicit, free-standing SEL goals and benchmarks, within which assessment and monitoring to demonstrate student progress are of course heavily encouraged (Dusenbury et al., 2011).

> **〰 Points for Reflection**
>
> • What challenges are posed by the need for routine outcome monitoring of SEL in schools?

It may be a belief that the kinds of constructs involved in SEL are difficult to evidence in a rigorous way – indeed, we received such feedback in our evaluation of the primary SEAL small group work element (Humphrey et al., 2008), where staff often felt that 'checklists' could not adequately capture subtle changes in children's behaviour that had come about as a result of their interventions. At a more fundamental level, the lack of routine assessment, monitoring and evaluation of SEL in schools may be a reflection of the power of 'faith over evidence' among practitioners who advocate these approaches. That is, we don't *need* to collect evidence because we *know* intuitively that SEL works. Indeed, I was once told this by a senior consultant to the Department for Education who had been working on the SEAL programme. However, given the heterogeneity of approaches to SEL and the cynicism with which it is viewed in some sectors of education, this is not an assumption that we can afford to make (Humphrey, 2012).

The topic of this chapter is also a crucial consideration for researchers, as the quality and range of the tools available for assessment, monitoring and evaluation of SEL clearly has implications for the subsequent credibility of studies published in the area that use said tools.

Key issues in assessing SEL

It is fair to say that the development of the assessment 'strand' of the broader field of SEL has lagged behind other areas. Indeed, 'there is a notable lack of good assessment instrumentation available that is designed exclusively with SEL competencies in mind' (Merrell and

Gueldner, 2010: 124). As evidence of this, consider the fact that in a recent systematic review of measures of social and emotional skills for children and young people (Humphrey et al., 2011), we found only 12 from over 200 identified that had any kind of reasonable 'shelf life'. That is, they had appeared in four or more academic journal articles, which we took to indicate they had moved beyond initial development and had started to be put to use by researchers. Even within these 12, many had no norms, and although most met basic psychometric criteria, few had been subject to more refined analysis (for example, analysis of differential item functioning). So the field is perhaps best described as 'emergent'. How is this reflected in the subsequent state of SEL evaluation research? Returning briefly to the major meta-analysis by Durlak et al. (2011), the authors reported that only 32 per cent of the studies reviewed assessed social and emotional skills as an outcome measure, 24 per cent used measures with no reported reliability and 49 per cent used measures with no reported validity. Such findings led the authors to conclude that 'there is a need for theory-driven research that not only aids in the accurate assessment of various skills but also identifies how different skills are related' (p. 419).

 Points for Reflection

- Why has the assessment strand of SEL lagged behind other areas such as programme development?

The parameters of SEL – what are we assessing?

We have seen already the importance of drawing clear parameters around constructs, and I have discussed issues pertaining to the lack of conceptual clarity for some aspects of SEL (see Chapter 2). Suffice it to say that these issues are magnified exponentially when we begin to consider assessment. Developmental taxonomies (for example, the aforementioned frameworks proposed by Denham and Brown, 2010, and Saarni, 1999) are helpful here, but attempting to align them to extant measures only serves to remind us that few, if any, well-validated measures actually capture the full gamut of domains of social and emotional competence (Merrell and Gueldner, 2010; Wigelsworth et al., 2010). Inspection of available measures also demonstrates just how much the heterogeneity evident in the operational definitions used by people influences the nature and content of instruments. So, for example, the Trait Emotional Intelligence Questionnaire (TEIQue) (Petrides and Furnham, 2001), based upon the extremely broad definition of EI noted in Chapter 2, contains items covering happiness, optimism, self-esteem and so on.

Scope and specificity are also important issues. At the broadest level, measures such as the aforementioned TEIQue (Petrides and Furnham, 2001) and the Emotional Literacy Assessment Instrument (ELAI) (Southampton Psychology Service, 2003) provide a single, uni-dimensional indicator of social and emotional competence. These types of measures tend to be short and easy to administer and score. However, they lack specificity and tend to be less 'change sensitive' than the more detailed, multi-dimensional measures that are available. This is an important consideration in evaluation, because it can mean that meaningful change can be missed if a given measure is not able to pinpoint it. An example of a multi-dimensional measure is the Social Skills Rating System (also known as the Social Skills Improvement System) (SSRS/SSIS) (Gresham and Elliot, 2008), which provides indicators of children's cooperation, assertiveness, responsibility, empathy and self-control. These types of measures provide a more detailed profile, but can be lengthier as a result. At the highest level of specificity, measures such as the Emotional Dysregulation Scale (EDS) (Penza et al., 1998) provide a single, uni-dimensional indicator of a specific social or emotional skill domain.

Methods of assessment

Merrell (2008; Merrell and Gueldner, 2010) suggests six key methods by which we may assess children and young people's social and emotional functioning. In the interests of brevity I have conflated rating scales and self-report assessment and therefore present five methods here. These are direct behavioural observation, rating scales, interviewing techniques, sociometric techniques and projective-expressive assessment techniques. These are by no means used in equal measure in SEL research though, with studies primarily relying on child self-report and/or parent or teacher informant report rating scales (Durlak et al., 2011). In Table 5.1 I provide a brief overview of each, some examples, and notes about their inherent strengths and weaknesses.

Table 5.1 Methods of assessment of SEL

Assessment method	Description	Example(s)	Key strengths	Key weaknesses
Rating scales (self and informant report)	Typically a series of statements (e.g. 'I know when I am getting angry') designed to reflect the constructs being measured (e.g. self-awareness), to which the respondent indicates a level of agreement or frequency (e.g. 1–5, with 5 being 'always', and 1 being 'never')	Social Skills Improvement System (Gresham and Elliot, 2008)	• Typically quick and easy to administer and score • Informant report versions can be used to assess children who may be unable to provide information about themselves • Information can be triangulated from multiple sources readily (e.g. child, teacher, parent)	• Can be subject to response bias and error variance • Ratings may not always correspond to observed behaviour
Direct behavioural observation	Specific behaviours of interest (e.g. physical aggression) are observed and systematically recorded (e.g. frequency, duration), typically in a natural setting (e.g. the playground). Each behaviour of interest has a clear working definition	Peer Interaction Observation Schedule (Pellegrini and Bartini, 2000)	• Considered to be perhaps the most objective assessment technique • Produces rich, systematic data across a range of contexts	• The 'observer reactivity effect' – the presence of an observer influences the behaviour of the subject • Time-consuming and expensive in comparison to other methods • Some aspects of children's social and emotional competence may be difficult to pinpoint in actual behavioural acts
Projective-expressive techniques	Use of creative methods such as drawing and storytelling, data from which is used to interpret children's social and emotional states (the underlying assumption being that children subconsciously project this through the task)	Kinetic Drawing System (Knoff and Prout, 1985)	• Can be more appealing to children than other methods (such as rating scales) • May yield insights into children's inner lives that are not directly accessible through other approaches	• Subjective and can be unreliable • Interpretation without additional corroborating evidence can raise ethical and legal issues

		Advantages	Disadvantages
Interviews	Discussion with an informant – for example, child, parent, teacher – in which key questions relating to SEL process and outcomes may be explored in depth. These discussions can range in both structure and formality. May also take the form of clinical interviews – in which specific information about a child's behaviour, mental health etc. may be elicited Semi-structured Clinical Interview for Children (McConaughy and Achenbach, 2001)	• Flexible approach that allows in-depth discussion of SEL issues • Interviewees have the opportunity to clarify understanding • Most useful way to gain insights into the lived experience of stakeholders in the SEL process	• Can be time-consuming, both in terms of administration and analysis • Can be difficult to garner a full range of opinions (e.g. responses may be skewed)
Sociometric techniques	Information pertaining to key social constructs – such as popularity and acceptance – is gathered through techniques that directly involve the individuals in a given social group. So, for example, all children in a class might be asked to rate or nominate each other according to a range of attributes (e.g. helpful, disruptive) or who they like (or don't like) to play with Social Inclusion Survey (Frederickson and Graham, 1999)	• Can elicit vital information about social behaviour that is difficult for adult observers to access • Can be strongly predictive of social-emotional outcomes	• Schools can be uncomfortable with certain approaches (e.g. in which children are asked to rate their classmates according to negative traits, such as being disruptive) • Peer ratings and nominations can be influenced by other factors, such as physical attractiveness, academic success and similarities in gender and ethnicity

Adapted in part from Merrell (2008).

The distinction between maximal and typical behavior

Among the approaches discussed in this chapter, a distinction between measures of typical and maximal behaviour needs to be drawn. Measures of *typical* behaviour are attained through rating scales (both self and informant report) which ask respondents to report on what they feel is 'usually the case' (for example, 'I am good at identifying other people's feelings'). Measures of *maximal* behaviour, however, require respondents to complete a task that actually taps the underlying construct in question (for example, respondents are shown a picture of a face and asked to describe how the person is feeling) (Wigelsworth et al., 2010). This is paralleled in the literature on emotional intelligence, with *trait* (akin to typical behaviour) and *ability* (akin to maximal behaviour) EI proposed as two distinct constructs (Mayer et al., 2008).

This schism in the assessment of social and emotional competence is a crucial one for a number of reasons. There is little doubt that the trait/typical and ability/maximal approaches measure different things – indeed, the correlation between them is only around 0.20 (which indicates about 4 per cent shared variance) (Davis and Humphrey, 2012a). Given this, which can be considered the more valid approach to assessment of SEL? Trait/typical measures (and their underlying constructs) have certainly come in for criticism among some experts in the field. For example, Mayer et al. (2008) remarked that their use 'reflects a lack of understanding . . . and undermines good scientific practice' (p. 513). Measures that use this approach, while considered advantageous in that they are easy and quick to administer and score, are subject to high levels of bias and social desirability.

Critics have also suggested that trait/typical measures essentially tap existing personality constructs rather than provide distinct information about actual social-emotional competence. This has been borne out in studies, with a clear association between the two (see, for example, Davis and Humphrey, 2012a). Such measures also typically draw from a much broader palette in terms of what is being assessed (see comments above regarding the content of the TEIQue), in the views of some making them 'preposterously all-encompassing' (Locke, 2005: 428). However, there is evidence that typical behaviour measures are in fact related to some real-world behavioural expressions that should be reflective of their social and emotional competence. For example, they correlate well with measures of children's peer relationships (Mavroveli et al., 2009; Petrides et al., 2006).

Maximal measures are considered to be more 'direct' measures of social and emotional competence (Wigelsworth et al., 2010).

However, they are much more time-consuming to administer and score, as many involve open coding (e.g. open-ended responses that the administrator is required to interpret) (Willhelm, 2005). Maximal measures also tend to be more restricted in scope, and there are few that come close to assessing the full gamut of social and emotional competencies. This is a particular issue for the domain of self-awareness, in which it is difficult to envisage how one might produce a maximal task (given that self-awareness is, by definition, an intra-personal skill). Finally, just as typical behaviour measures have been criticised for their overlap with personality traits, maximal measures have been found to correlate positively with general cognitive ability (Davis and Humphrey, 2012a).

In the SEL evaluation literature, outcome measurement is usually conducted using typical behaviour measures (with some notable exceptions – see, for example, Greenberg et al., 1995). In some cases they are used in combination, with interesting results. In our evaluation of the primary SEAL small group work element in England (Humphrey et al., 2008), we were able to administer both typical (the ELAI – Southampton Psychology Service, 2003) and maximal (the Kusche Affective Inventory – Greenberg and Kusche, 1993 – and the Child Role Play Measure – Dodge et al., 1985) measures in a small number of participating schools. The former produced some evidence of significant changes as a result of participation in SEAL small group work, but the latter did not. This raises the question as to which assessment protocol should be given priority in determining whether a given intervention has been 'successful'.

Who provides information?

Assessment, monitoring and evaluation data in relation to SEL is typically sourced from children themselves, their parents, teachers/school staff and peers. Each of these 'informants' can provide a unique perspective, and hence multi-informant evaluation is to be encouraged.

Children and young people

As already noted, having children rate their own social and emotional competence is the most popular approach in the SEL literature (Durlak et al., 2011). Merrell (2008) states that child self-report can 'provide unique and valuable information as part of a broad-based assessment design' (p. 199), and the approach is advantageous for several reasons.

Firstly, through introspection, the child has access to the most detailed information about him/herself of any of the possible respondents. From a purely pragmatic point of view, using child self-report is also often the simplest way of obtaining a large enough data sample for a rigorous profiling or evaluation exercise. More broadly, the approach is also in line with the increasing push to take children's perspectives into account.

However, there are also limitations to this approach. Firstly, children's self-awareness follows a developmental trajectory. Older children and adolescents, with their heightened self-awareness and increasingly differentiated self-concept, are therefore likely to be more accurate responders than younger children (Denham et al., 2009). This issue is true for child self-report measurement in other areas. However, it is particularly pertinent here, given that self-awareness itself is commonly included as a domain in measures of social and emotional competence. These kinds of measures also contain several potential sources of bias, including acquiescence (the tendency to answer items consistently in one direction), social desirability (where the respondent endorses items in a manner which portrays socially desirable traits), faking (deliberate attempts to manipulate one's response pattern to create a particular effect) and deviation (the propensity to respond to items in unusual ways) (Merrell, 2008).

Parents and carers

The parent informant report method carries the advantage of providing a unique window into a child's behaviour at home (Wigelsworth et al., 2010). With regard to SEL evaluations, parents are also arguably less susceptible to the potential response bias that can occur with ratings provided by children and/or their teachers, who may inflate scores because of their enjoyment or interest in a given intervention as opposed to meaningful social, emotional or behavioural change. However, they also typically have a much more restricted frame of reference when completing measures than do teachers. Parents are also harder to recruit and retain in studies, and there is evidence that those of children considered to be at risk (Esbensen et al., 1999) may be greatly under-represented in studies.

Teachers and other school staff

Another option is to use teachers or other school staff to provide ratings. Teachers benefit from seeing a given child's behaviour in school and can also use their collective experience with other children as a frame of reference in completing measures. This means a teacher-rated measure of social and emotional competence can have greater discriminative power than other approaches (Humphrey et al., 2008). However, teacher education and experience can influence ratings. For instance, more experienced teachers tend to give children higher ratings (Denham, 2005). From experience, it can also be a challenge to persuade school staff of the benefits of completing the same measure for every child in their class, and even when this is achieved, issues of fatigue effects and consequent loss of sensitivity need to be considered.

Problematic issues that are relevant to both teacher *and* parent informant ratings of social and emotional competence include response bias due to halo effects (where a child is rated in a positive or negative way as a result of a characteristic that is not directly relevant to what is being measured), leniency or severity (tending to be overly generous or harsh in ratings) and central tendency effects (consistently selecting the 'midpoint'). There are also several sources of error variance, including those caused by the setting (for example, a child may behave one way at home and a different way in class) and the passage of time (during which children's behaviour will change) (Merrell, 2008).

Peers

One alternative approach to assessment in this area, advocated by Frederickson and Cline (2009), is the use of peer ratings, including sociometry. In a typical example, children are given descriptions (for example, of cooperative behaviour) and are asked to 'guess who?' from their classmates (Coie et al., 1982). An alternative approach involves children being given a list of their classmates and asked to rate each of them on relevant attributes, from which social status and social-behavioural characteristics can be derived (Merrell, 2008). Peer-rated methods are considered useful in assessing social skills because 'the social behaviour of older pupils, in particular, is relatively complex and private, making it difficult for adult observers to make reliable and representative observations. Peers may have better access to low frequency but psychologically meaningful events that lead to the establishment of social reputations' (Frederickson and Cline, 2009: 476). However, peer-rated approaches are less well established in relation to assessing emotional competence, and are known to be influenced by personal attributes such as physical attractiveness and academic success. Furthermore, interactive factors such as similarities in gender and race may also skew results (Frederickson and Cline,

2009). Finally, from personal experience, schools can sometimes object to the use of these methods if they feel that the process may reinforce or exacerbate the social status of unpopular or rejected children.

〰️ **Points for Reflection**

- In the event of differential findings from a multi-informant assessment of a given SEL intervention, whose perspective should be prioritised and why?

Taken together, it is clear that no single respondent or assessment technique alone can provide flawless information. This reinforces the need – wherever possible – to use multi-informant, multi-source data in the assessment and monitoring of SEL. Although this invariably incurs additional costs in terms of time, human resources and complexity, the insights yielded can be powerful. For example, in our evaluation of the primary SEAL small group work element in England, we found positive changes in outcomes among children selected for intervention according to our self-report and teacher informant-report measures, but not from our parent informant-report measures. This suggested to us that the children may not have been generalising or applying the skills they had developed in the small-group setting beyond the immediate school environment, and on this basis we recommended that future iterations of the interventions should include a more explicit parental/familial component (Humphrey et al., 2008).

Cultural issues

As we saw in Chapter 2, prevailing definitions of SEL carry with them assumptions about what it means to be socially and emotionally competent that may not take into account cultural differences in emotional development, experience and expression. The same problem raises its head here – indeed, the notion of cultural *biases* in the area of educational assessment more generally has been the subject of considerable controversy for some time (see, for example, Herrnstein and Murray, 1994).

A fundamental issue is that, on the one hand, there has been rapidly increasing cultural diversification in education systems across the world as a result of ethnic migration (Merrell and Gueldner,

2010). Consider, for example, that in a school in Manchester, England (where I live and work), the first language of pupils may be Albanian, Arabic, Czech, Katchi, Kurdish, Latvian, Malay, Punjabi, Polish, Persian, Somali, Urdu, Yoruba, etc. The diversity of pupils' languages, along with their traditions, customs, values and beliefs, is something to be celebrated and can be a valuable educational tool for promoting tolerance and acceptance of difference.

However, with only a few exceptions, the various approaches to SEL assessment outlined in this chapter have been designed by and validated on a much more homogenous, Anglo-American population (Merrell, 2008). Indeed, in our aforementioned systematic review of measures of social and emotional competence (Humphrey et al., 2011), we found that although many measures were available in a variety of languages, there was little evidence of any attempt to assess the applicability of instruments to children from different ethnic groups. The one exception we were able to find to this – the SSIS (Gresham and Elliot, 2008) – demonstrates the importance of this consideration. Van Horn et al.'s (2007) analysis of this instrument with samples of African American, Caucasian and Hispanic children in the United States demonstrated that it may not assess the same construct over time in these different groups. Hence, the authors proposed culturally specific corrections to the basic factor structure and scoring system.

Merrell (2008) outlines a range of other critical issues pertaining to cultural differences and the assessment and monitoring of SEL, including the need for the professional/researcher to be culturally competent (for example, knowledgeable about cultural values that may impact upon children's behavioural expression in certain contexts). He also notes the parallel need to recognise the dangers inherent in focusing upon or emphasising groups or categories when talking about cultural issues, suggesting that such discourses actively reinforce stereotypes of minority groups. That is, if we consistently talk about the need to respect the cultural values of 'Asian children', for example, we homogenise them in doing so and fail to recognise that they are individuals who vary in the extent to which they adopt such values in their daily lives.

Psychometric properties

This is a fundamental consideration – any given assessment instrument needs to demonstrate that it measures with consistency (that is, it is reliable) and that it actually measures what it is intended to measure (that is, it is valid). Notwithstanding the aforementioned issues regarding scope and specificity, it is fair to say that many available measures in this field demonstrate acceptable psychometric properties using standard techniques (for example, internal consistency, test-retest reliability, factorial validity, discriminative validity) (Wigelsworth et al., 2010). However, evidence relating to more advanced analysis (such as those based upon Item Response Theory – as recommended by Terwee et al., 2007) is still lacking for most measures (with some notable exceptions, such as the Matson Evaluation of Social Skills in Youngsters (MESSY) (Matson et al., 1983).

In spite of the inarguable importance of the psychometric properties of available instruments, there is variability in the extent to which this issue is highlighted for schools. So, for example, in the assessment and monitoring guidance produced for schools in relation to the SEAL programme in England (Department for Education and Skills, 2007b), no mention was made of issues of reliability or validity, and of the variety of instruments recommended, only one (the School Emotional Environment for Learning Survey) (Haddon et al., 2005) had been formally evaluated in this regard. However, other guides, such as the compendium of SEL measures published by CASEL (Denham et al., 2010) pay due attention to such issues.

A selected anthology of measures of social and emotional competence in children and young people

As noted earlier, the number of available measures of social and emotional competence is overwhelming. The number of well-validated instruments that have a decent 'shelf life' in terms of their continued use in research is much shorter. In this section I provide a brief, selective overview of some of the instruments that have been widely used in the literature, in addition to a couple of more recently developed measures. I have included both typical and maximal behaviour measures. Available space does not permit a more comprehensive review. For this, interested readers may wish to refer to our work at Manchester (Humphrey et al., 2011; Wigelsworth et al., 2010) and that of others in the field, including Kenneth Merrell (Merrell, 2008; Merrell and Gueldner, 2010), Susanne Denham (Denham et al., 2009; Denham et al., 2010) and CASEL (http://www.casel.org).

Points for Reflection

- What are some of the key practical considerations in selecting an appropriate SEL measure?

Social Skills Improvement System (formerly the Social Skills Rating System)

The SSIS (Gresham and Elliot, 2008) is a measure of typical (as opposed to maximal) behaviour that is used to assess social and emotional competence of children and young people aged 3–18. It utilises a rating scale format, in which respondents read a statement (for example, '[This child] shows concern for others') and indicate their level of agreement on a four-point scale. It has child self-report (age 8 upwards) and parent and teacher informant-report versions (all ages). The domains of children's social and emotional competence assessed via the SSIS are communication, cooperation, assertion, responsibility, empathy, engagement and self-control. These can be combined to form a composite 'social skills' measure. Items pertaining to competing problem behaviours (externalising, bullying, hyperactivity/inattention, internalising, autism spectrum) and academic competence (reading achievement, maths achievement, motivation to learn) are also included. It is quite a lengthy scale, with 75–83 items in total (depending upon the version used), and can take in excess of 25 minutes to complete.

The SSIS is well established in the literature, having been included in upwards of 40 published articles, and has excellent psychometric properties, meeting standard reliability (internal, test-retest, inter-rater) and validity (factorial, convergent, discriminative) requirements. It has also been subjected to analysis of differential item functioning. This allows researchers to examine, for example, whether children from different ethnic groups with the same latent skill respond differently to particular items. The instrument is norm referenced, but those norms are for a US population only.

Key strengths and weaknesses of the SSIS:

+ Comprehensive coverage of domains of SEL, in addition to other relevant domains
+ Multi-informant versions available

+   Strong psychometric properties
–   Only normed for US population
–   Lengthy compared to other measures

Emotional Quotient Inventory – Youth Version

The EQi-YV (Bar-On and Parker, 2008) is a measure of trait emotional intelligence (akin to a 'typical behaviour' measure of social and emotional competence) for children and young people aged 7–18. It also utilises a rating scale format, in which respondents read a statement (for example, 'I can talk easily about my feelings') and indicate their level of agreement on a four-point scale. The EQi-YV only uses child self-report. There are currently no informant-report versions. The domains covered in the EQi-YV are children's intrapersonal competence, interpersonal competence, stress management, adaptability and general mood. There are also two respondent validity scales, which give an indication of any inconsistency in responses and evidence of attempts to create an overly positive impression. The full length version of the EQi-YV includes 60 items (taking up to 20 minutes to complete). A short version containing only 30 (taking less than 10 minutes) can also be administered. The trade-off with the latter is that the number of domains measured is curtailed. The EQi-YV is norm-referenced, with both US and UK norms.

In terms of psychometric properties, the developers of the EQi-YV have demonstrated its internal consistency and test-retest reliability, and subsequently produced standard errors of measurement and prediction by age and gender. They have also demonstrated the factorial and construct validity of the measure (Bar-On and Parker, 2008). Additionally, research has also demonstrated the predictive and discriminative utility of the EQi-YV (e.g. Parker et al., 2004).

Key strengths and weaknesses of the EQi-YV:

+   Positive impression and inconsistency index
+   Short version available
+   Has both US and UK norms
–   Self-report only
–   Broader domains lack specificity (e.g. intrapersonal competence conflates self-awareness and self-management)

Assessment of Children's Emotional Skills

The ACES (Schultz et al., 2004) is a maximal behaviour measure of children's emotional understanding. Specifically, it assesses their emotion attribution accuracy and emotion biases. It is for use with children aged 4–8, and is divided into three sections which deal with facial expressions, social behaviours and social situations respectively. Taking 10–25 minutes to complete, it comprises 26 photos of faces and 30 short sentences covering social behaviours and situations. Children are required to label the facial expression, described behaviour or described social situation from a limited number of possible responses (e.g. 'Does this face look happy, mad, sad, scared or no feeling?'). Scores on each domain reflect the extent to which children are able to attribute emotions accurately. As a maximal measure, the ACES does not have informant-report versions. The measure demonstrates adequate internal consistency and predictive validity (Mavroveli et al., 2009).

Key strengths and weaknesses of the ACES:

+ Maximal measure, so provides a more 'direct' assessment
+ Closed scoring, unlike many maximal measures
- No norms
- Fairly narrow in terms of coverage of domains of SEL

Mayer-Salovey-Caruso Emotional Intelligence Test – Youth Version

The MSCEIT-YV (Mayer et al., in press) is a measure of ability emotional intelligence (akin to a maximal behaviour measure of social and emotional competence). It is technically still in development, but a research version is available from the developers of the instrument. The MSCEIT-YV was developed for use with children and young people aged 10–18. It takes approximately 45 minutes to complete and contains 101 items that assess respondents' skills in perceiving emotion, using emotion to facilitate thought, understanding emotion and management of emotions. A variety of tasks are used to generate scores in each of these areas. For example, perceiving emotion is assessed by showing respondents a series of faces which they rate for emotional content on a five-point scale. The MSECIT-YV scores are derived from expert consensus. That is, individual scores are assigned a degree of 'correctness' based upon how closely they match the answers considered appropriate by a panel of experts in the field of emotion.

Initial analysis of the psychometric properties of the MSCEIT-YV indicate that it demonstrates acceptable split-half reliability and construct and predictive validity (Davis and Humphrey, 2012a; Peters et al., 2009). Further analyses are likely to be published once the instrument is officially published.

Key strengths and weaknesses of the MSCEIT-YV:

+ The most comprehensive maximal measure currently available
+ Strong theoretical underpinnings (based upon Salovey and Mayer's (1990) model of emotional intelligence)
− Unsuitable for children in primary/elementary education
− Lengthy to administer and score (indeed, at present responses must be scored by the publisher)

Social-Emotional Assets and Resilience Scales

The SEARS (Merrell and Gueldner, 2010) is a recently published typical behaviour SEL measure for children and young people aged 5–18. Like the other typical behaviour measures featured here, it utilises a rating scale format, in which respondents read a statement (for example, 'I stay calm when there is a problem or argument') and indicate their level of agreement on a four-point scale. The SEARS provides measures of self-regulation, social competence, empathy and responsibility, in addition to a composite score made up of each of these four sub-scales. It has child self-report (age 8 upwards) and teacher and parent informant-report (all ages) versions. Separate scales are available for children (ages 8–12) and adolescents (ages 13–18). The various scales vary in length between 35 and 41 items. Like the EQi-YV, a short form containing just 12 items is also available, although this only produces a single 'resiliency' score. The SEARS has strong psychometric properties (Merrell et al., 2010) and has been shown to be 'change sensitive' (Merrell and Gueldner, 2010).

Key strengths and weaknesses of the SEARS:

+ Designed with SEL in mind and so provides a close match to key domains
+ Strengths-based rather than problem-focused

+   Separate scales for children and adolescents, reflecting different reading and developmental levels
−   US norms only

Beyond social and emotional competence – what else should be assessed?

The primary focus of this chapter has been on the assessment of social and emotional competence since this is the primary proximal outcome of SEL programmes. However, it should also be acknowledged that there are other variables that can and should be monitored – but where do we start? The SEL logic model (see Chapter 2) is helpful here. It reminds us that another proximal outcome of SEL is an improved classroom or school climate (manifest by feelings of safety, being cared for and so on). Given this, it is surprising how few studies have actually examined this as an outcome in SEL evaluations. A potential difficulty is that of the variety of measures available – most have not been developed with SEL in mind and may therefore lack the focus on specific social and emotional aspects of school climate where we might expect to see some change. That said, there are some useful measures available, including the School as a Caring Community Profile (SCCP) (Battistich et al., 1995). This was developed in the US but used in the UK and elsewhere (e.g. Humphrey et al., 2010). The SCCP surveys pupils' *trust and respect for teachers, liking for school, perceptions of classroom and school supportiveness* and *feelings of autonomy and influence*. Children respond to a series of statements about their school and indicate their agreement on a four-point rating scale (an example item is 'I like my school'). The SCCP has good internal consistency and face validity.

As we move through the stages of the SEL logic model (and the associated literature on SEL, e.g. Durlak et al., 2011), other more distal variables are evident that are also strong candidates for assessment and monitoring. These include learners':

• attitudes towards and feelings of attachment to school;

• pro-social behaviour;

• mental health, such as anxiety, depression and conduct problems (see Wolpert et al. (2008) for a recent systematic review of measures for children and young people);

• school outcomes – academic performance, attendance, exclusions.

Available space does not permit a full and detailed discussion of each of these. However, as most can be measured in similar ways to social and emotional skills, the range of issues outlined above apply equally here. Additionally, given that these outcome variables are manifestations of more distal effects of SEL, it is important to note that expectations of the magnitude of change need to be adjusted accordingly. Put simply, we expect less movement in these areas as a result of SEL. Given that it is a 'downstream' effect, such change might also take longer to emerge.

Further Reading

Denham, S., Ji, P. and Hamre, B. (2010) *Compendium of Preschool Through Elementary School Social-Emotional Learning and Associated Assessment Measures.* Chicago: CASEL/University of Illinois.

Humphrey, N., Kalambouka, A., Wigelsworth, M., Lendrum, A., Wolpert, M. and Aitken, J. (2011) 'A systematic review of measures of social and emotional skills in children and young people', *Educational and Psychological Measurement*, 70: 617–37.

Merrell, K. (2008) *Behavioural, Social and Emotional Assessment of Children and Adolescents.* London: Routledge.

Implementation

Overview

The aim of this chapter is to explore the implementation of approaches to SEL. I begin with a rationale for the study of implementation, before outlining and discussing different aspects such as fidelity, dosage and participant responsiveness. There is an emphasis on research findings that highlight the influence of each of these on study outcomes. The chapter continues with an examination of the factors affecting implementation, such as school leadership and implementer characteristics, before concluding with a look at Domitrovich et al.'s (2008) conceptual framework for maximising implementation quality.

Key Points

- Implementation is the process by which an intervention is put into practice.
- Understanding implementation is vital for several reasons, not least of which is the evidence that implementation variability can influence outcomes.
- There are several different aspects of implementation but the majority of research in the field has focused solely on fidelity/adherence and dosage.

- Studies examining the influence of implementation on intervention outcomes have produced some mixed findings. This variability appears to stem from methodological factors such as:
  — which aspect(s) of implementation are assessed;
  — by whom (e.g. teacher self-report versus independent observation);
  — when and how often measures of implementation are taken.
- There are a variety of factors that affect the implementation of a given intervention, including:
  — preplanning and foundations – such as the perceived need for change;
  — implementation support system – such as the provision of training;
  — implementation environment – such as leadership support;
  — implementer factors – such as teachers' attitudes toward SEL;
  — programme characteristics – such as the component structure.

Implementation matters

The importance of implementation cannot be overstated. Research in this area has yielded major insights that have helped to develop our understanding of *how* and *why* educational interventions (including SEL programmes) work (Carroll et al., 2007; Durlak, 2010). Durlak and DuPre (2008) have suggested that implementation 'refers to what a programme consists of when it is delivered in a particular setting' (p. 329). In Raudenbush's (2008) terms, it is therefore about the *enactment* of a given *instructional regime*, that is the process by which an intervention is actually put into practice.

Why is this process considered to be so significant? Firstly, it is because research studies across multiple disciplines have consistently demonstrated that interventions are rarely implemented as designed. Secondly, research has also shown that variability in implementation can be related to variability in the achievement of expected outcomes (Lendrum and Humphrey, 2012; Carroll et al., 2007). For example, Dix et al. (2012) demonstrated that the quality of implementation of the KidsMatter initiative in Australia (see Chapter 4) affected subsequent academic outcomes for students.

Domitrovich and Greenberg (2000) offer several additional reasons as to why it is important for us to consider implementation:

1. Without implementation information it is impossible to know exactly what happened in an intervention.
2. Implementation information is essential in order to establish the internal validity of an intervention and to strengthen conclusions about its role in changing outcomes.
3. Implementation information helps us understand the intervention better – how different elements fit together, how users (e.g. trainers, implementers and participants) interact, and so on.
4. Implementation information can be used to provide ongoing feedback that can enhance subsequent delivery.
5. Implementation information can advance knowledge on how best to replicate programme effects in real-world settings (e.g. when a 'proven' intervention is brought to scale).

The study of implementation has developed as researchers have begun to understand its importance. This is evident in the number of evaluation studies in which it has been considered in some way. In an early review, Durlak (1997) found that only 5 per cent of studies of preventive interventions provided data on implementation. By the time of the same author's meta-analysis of universal SEL programmes 14 years later (Durlak et al., 2011), this figure had risen to 57 per cent. However, this still leaves just under half of the evaluation studies in the field where the focus has been solely on outcomes. As Domitrovich et al. (2008) state, 'the research base on implementation quality is not keeping pace with the growing emphasis on adoption of empirically derived interventions' (p. 18).

This chapter will examine different elements of implementation, the factors that moderate them and the relationship between the two. Throughout I will also make reference to research that signifies the downstream effects of all of this on the achievement of intended outcomes.

〰️ **Points for Reflection**

*   Why has research on the implementation of SEL programmes taken so long to gain prominence in the field?

Elements of implementation

There have been numerous attempts to describe and classify the different aspects of implementation that can be studied (e.g. Carroll et al., 2007; Durlak and DuPre, 2008; Greenberg et al., 2005). The elements common to most are outlined in Table 6.1.

Table 6.1   Different elements in the study of implementation

Aspect of implementation	Description	Practical example
Fidelity	The extent to which a school is adhering to the intended treatment model	How faithfully a school replicates the prescribed activities and principles described in the programme guidance
Dosage	How much of the intervention has been delivered	A class teacher only manages to deliver 15 of the total 25 lessons in a given programme to her class
Quality	How well different components of an intervention are delivered	How well prepared a teacher is to deliver a given session, and/or the energy, confidence and enthusiasm with which they deliver it
Participant responsiveness	The degree to which children and their parents engage with the intervention	Whether children and parents complete home extension activities
Programme differentiation	The extent to which intervention activities can be distinguished from other, existing practice	The conceptual and pedagogic similarity between sessions on resolving conflict in an SEL intervention and existing lessons taught as part of students' personal, social and health education
Programme reach	The rate and scope of participation	A school decides to deliver a universal intervention in targeted, small-group sessions for children perceived to be 'at risk' of developing difficulties
Adaptation	The nature and extent of changes made to the intervention (which can be 'surface' or 'deep')	Substituting or changing prescribed role play exercise in a given session in order to draw links to other work that the class had been doing in the formal academic curriculum
Monitoring of control/comparison conditions	Determining what SEL-related activities are taking place at the sites with which intervention schools are being compared	In a study examining the efficacy of SEL intervention A, some comparison schools start to implement SEL intervention B

Adapted from Carroll et al. (2007), Durlak and DuPre (2008) and Greenberg et al. (2005).

Before discussing each of these elements in turn, some general issues are worthy of note. Firstly, although they are presented as distinct, there is a significant degree of overlap between these different elements. So, for example, fidelity is often used as an umbrella term that incorporates others, such as dosage and reach (see, for example, Carroll et al., 2007; Century et al., 2010). Such overlaps notwithstanding, the different aspects of implementation are expected to be distinct but related with one another. So, for example, in a school where programme differentiation is an issue because existing practice is very similar to the intervention being adopted, participant responsiveness may be lower than in a similar school with relatively less developed SEL practices because the programme does not add as much that can be seen as new or unique.

How do we assess implementation?

A set of related issues are which aspects of implementation are assessed, how they are assessed and by whom. In the field of SEL, it is fair to say that certain elements noted above have predominated – in particular, fidelity/adherence and dosage (Durlak and DuPre, 2008). This may be because they are perceived to be easier to measure than other, potentially more complicated aspects such as programme differentiation. Hence, elements of implementation beyond fundamental notions of fidelity and dosage can provide critical information and therefore must be considered in order to provide a comprehensive analysis.

In terms of how implementation is assessed, both quantitative and qualitative indicators can be extremely useful. With a few exceptions (e.g. Social and Character Development Research Consortium, 2010), quantitative assessment of implementation has tended to be programme-specific, with bespoke measurement protocols developed to match individual interventions. For example, in the evaluation of the KidsMatter initiative in Australia, the researchers developed an Implementation Index that was used to assess fidelity, dosage and quality of implementation (Dix et al., 2010, 2012; Slee et al., 2009). Similarly, the PATHS curriculum in the US has its own 'implementation rubric' with accompanying surveys and observation schedules.

Quantitative assessment of elements of implementation can be extremely useful in the sense that it can be statistically modelled against outcomes, but they can also provide an overly simplistic picture of the complex processes at play. Qualitative assessment of implementation processes – such as interviews with key stakeholders, observations in a range of contexts and document review – can yield important insights that help to put 'flesh on the bones' of the quantitative data gathered. They can also be particularly useful in exploratory studies and/or where quantitative methods are not feasible or appropriate. In our evaluation of the secondary SEAL programme in England, the flexible nature of the intervention meant that any attempt to quantify implementation was likely to be redundant, and hence we conducted longitudinal, qualitative case studies of nine schools (Humphrey et al., 2010). These case studies provided rich, detailed information about each school's approach and the barriers to and facilitators of effective implementation that quantitative measures would doubtlessly have missed. For example, our interviews revealed that while many staff welcomed the flexible nature of the SEAL framework, they also found that it left them without a clear 'road map' for implementation (Lendrum et al., 2012). Hence qualitative methods can serve a powerful explanatory function that helps us to understand both implementation and subsequent outcomes. In this example, it meant that we were able to understand why implementation stalled in many schools and hence why our assessment of outcomes produced null results.

The sources of information about implementation are also vitally important. Broadly speaking, there are two key sources – the self-reports of implementers (e.g. school staff) and independent observations (Domitrovich et al., 2008). Although few studies have directly compared these two strategies (Durlak and DuPre, 2008), those that have highlight two important issues. Firstly, although data from implementer self-reports and independent observations tend to be correlated, the former typically report higher levels of implementation than the latter. It is unclear whether these more optimistic ratings are due to impression management, demand effects, differences in understanding of key aspects of the implementation requirements of a given intervention or some combination of each of these. Secondly, data from the latter are much more closely aligned with programme outcomes (Domitrovich et al., 2010a), with implementer self-reports not being significantly associated with outcome measures in some studies (e.g. Goldberg Lillehoj et al., 2004; Social and Character Development Research Consortium, 2010).

A related issue in terms of the assessment of implementation is how many 'measures' one should take in order to gain an optimal picture of the process (Domitrovich et al., 2010). One study looked at single and dual assessments and found that averaged ratings from two time points were more strongly associated with outcomes than a single measurement (Resnicow et al., 1998). We also know that the act of assessing implementation itself can influence programme outcomes. For example, Smith et al.'s (2004) review of school-wide anti-bullying programmes found that those in which implementation was systematically monitored yielded greater effect sizes on measured outcomes than those where it was not considered. Such an effect may be a result of changes in implementer behaviour. Hence, school staff may implement an intervention with greater fidelity when they know they are going to be observed or have to report on their activities during the course of implementation. Alternatively, it may reflect systemic differences between programmes. That is, implementation monitoring may be standard for some programmes because of the emphasis placed on fidelity by developers or because the structure and content of the programmes lend themselves to straightforward implementation measurement techniques.

A final issue worthy of note is how many different aspects of implementation should be assessed. As noted above, fidelity/adherence and dosage are the most commonly utilised measures. However, if a study measures only adherence and dosage, it may be tempting to conclude that implementation failure in either of these areas is causal if there are poor outcomes. In fact, these may be more accurately attributed to an aspect that has not been measured, such as quality or participant responsiveness. Similarly, if not all aspects of implementation are considered, and dosage and adherence are measured as high, poor outcomes may be incorrectly seen as programme/theory failure (e.g. a 'Type III error'). Hence, consideration of as many different elements of implementation as possible is vital.

Fidelity/adherence

A useful definition of fidelity/adherence is provided by Century et al. (2010), who state that it refers to 'the extent to which critical components of an intended program are presented when that program is enacted' (p. 202). This is a useful starting point because it introduces the notion of 'critical components', that is the building blocks of an intervention that are considered essential. What is 'essential' versus merely 'desirable' can be determined by reviewing written programme materials, talking to programme developers and/or engaging in user reviews with implementers (Century et al., 2010). It can also be done in a 'post-hoc' fashion by examining the results of studies that have modelled the presence/absence of different components against programme outcomes.

This approach fits well with the aforementioned observations that implementers always adapt a given programme in some way and that absolute fidelity is not always necessary to produce positive outcomes (Durlak and DuPre, 2008). Century et al. (2010) distinguish between *structural* and *instructional* critical components. The former refers to the design and organisation of the programme itself. Structural-procedural components are those that communicate what the implementer needs to do, typically exemplified in an intervention manual. Using the metaphor of food preparation in a restaurant, we might think of this as a step-by-step recipe that a chef needs to follow. Structural-educative components are essentially about what the skills (e.g. teaching approaches) and understanding (e.g. of the concepts being taught) are required on the part of the implementer, which may take the form of training requirements. Extending the food analogy, this could be thought of in terms of the training and experience a chef needs and makes use of when he/she prepares a dish.

It has become a truism that in SEL implementation, 'fidelity is king' in terms of securing better outcomes for students. In a similar vein, lack of fidelity is reported to be disastrous. Melde et al. (2006), for example, state 'the failure to provide programs as intended by program developers has proven time and time again to have dire consequences' (p. 716). The research in this field broadly backs up this viewpoint, but there are inconsistencies evident. So, while several studies have found clear associations between observational ratings of implementation fidelity and subsequent outcomes, others have not (Domitrovich et al., 2010a). In one study (Sánchez et al., 2007), increased fidelity was actually associated with *worse* outcomes! Several issues may be contributing to this rather confusing picture. Firstly, the number of fidelity observations taken in different studies may have varied, and as already noted, this can affect the relationship to outcomes. Secondly, if fidelity is high across different implementation settings (e.g. classrooms/schools), this produces a smaller range of scores, making it harder to establish links with outcomes (Domitrovich et al., 2010a). Finally, the relationship between fidelity and outcomes may simply depend upon the type of outcome and how it is measured. For example, one might expect a more robust association between SEL implementation fidelity and a proximal outcome such as children's social and emotional competence than with a more distal outcome such as academic progress. However, the aforementioned study by Dix et al. (2012) would seem to suggest that this is not always the case.

Points for Reflection

- What are the potential limitations of an overwhelming emphasis on fidelity/adherence?

Despite the clear importance of implementation fidelity in determining programme outcomes, the 'privileged status' it has achieved in the literature does raise some problematic issues. First and foremost is the tension this creates with adaptation. One the one hand, we know evidence-based SEL interventions need to be delivered as designed/intended in order to increase the likelihood of positive evaluation outcomes being replicated. However, such interventions also need to be responsive to local context and need, because otherwise the level of 'buy-in' is likely to be low (Castro et al., 2004). Related to this, a second issue is that the strong emphasis on fidelity may be seen as eroding professional autonomy among school staff (Humphrey, 2012). Furthermore, as already noted there is some inconsistency in the literature with the way in which the term fidelity is applied – as an umbrella term that incorporates other aspects of implementation or as a distinct entity in its own right. In some contexts it is used almost interchangeably with 'quality' (Domitrovich and Greenberg, 2000). This may further exacerbate existing tensions in relation to adaptation, since it would seem to imply that any adaptation inherently reduces quality. Finally, there are conceptual objections to the preponderance of extreme notions of fidelity in the SEL discourse. The nature of these objections are eloquently portrayed by Dixon (2012) in his satirical ponderings about how a modern-day Gradgrind (a character in Charles Dickens' *Hard Times* who embodies a purely rationalist approach to human experience) might approach SEL:

> He would seek, from any programme of emotional education,
> a package of activities that could be mechanically, identically,
> practiced in every classroom in the land, regardless of the fanciful
> foibles of individual teachers or the cultural inheritance of
> individual children . . . he would thus impose a single pedagogical
> scheme and a universal emotional language. (p. 12)

Adaptation

Adaptation shares a somewhat uncomfortable relationship with fidelity/adherence (see above) inasmuch as it is often seen as its diametric opposite and therefore by definition *not a good thing*. However, for at least some types of adaptation, research has shown that not only is it not necessarily damaging, but that it can in fact be very useful (Durlak, 2010). As already noted, some adaptation is inevitable, particularly when SEL interventions are brought to scale, and we know that 100 per cent fidelity is not a prerequisite for positive outcomes. Thus, we might ask, why does adaptation occur, and what is the effect of different kinds of adaptations on outcomes?

Adaptation may occur for a number of reasons, and may be categorised as intentional or unintentional, and proactive or reactive (Lendrum, 2010). At a basic level, teachers (who are often the 'implementers' in universal SEL programmes) like to establish a sense of ownership through adaptation. That is, they put their own 'stamp' on an intervention. Related to this, recognition of the fact that there is no 'one size fits all' approach means that adaptations may be made in order to increase the relevance of an intervention to local contexts. Castro et al. (2004) provide several examples of where mismatches between the groups with which an intervention was validated and a subsequent consumer group may give rise to essential adaptations, including language, socio-economic status, urbanicity, presence and severity of risk factors, and family stability. In the context of implementation of interventions in real-world settings, adaptation may also occur because implementers do not have access to resources that were present when a given programme was validated (for example, access to training and/or technical support and assistance). There may also be a lack of understanding of what are the critical components of the programme itself (see previous subsection). Finally, adaptation may also occur as a reaction to barriers to implementation outlined in the second half of this chapter.

Broadly speaking, there are two main types of adaptation – 'surface' and 'deep' – and these have divergent effects on outcomes (Lendrum, 2010). Surface adaptations involve relatively minor changes to an intervention and may include changing language (e.g. translating vocabulary), replacing images in programme content to provide a better match to a target audience, and substituting cultural references (Connor et al., 2007). These may strengthen positive outcomes because of the increased ownership of the intervention and its perceived relevance in a given school context. 'Deep' adaptations, on the other hand, involve more substantial modifications, such as reducing the number or length of sessions, removing topics/components or using staff who have not been trained to deliver the intervention (Connor et al., 2007). These are considered to be much riskier and are likely to reduce the effectiveness of a given intervention because they may affect the mechanism(s) through which change occurs.

Given the above, SEL intervention developers should assume that some adaptation is going to occur and perhaps pre-empt this by building some limited opportunities for flexible delivery into their intended model. This might include, for example, providing parallel sessions (e.g. equivalent versions of a lesson designed to promote awareness of other people's perspectives that have the same ultimate objectives but contrasting pedagogical approaches) or opportunities to substitute narratives/short stories provided in lesson outlines with equivalent texts that are part of a given school's reading scheme. Such opportunities would presumably bring the benefits attributed to increased flexibility, such as an increased likelihood of adoption, a greater sense of ownership and sustainability, and increased feelings of professional autonomy and agency, but within a framework that is still ultimately under the auspices of the developer.

A further implication is that implementers need to be made aware of how a given SEL programme works, the role of key components and which elements must be implemented as prescribed in order for change to occur. In practical terms, this puts the onus on programme developers to clarify their programme theory when implementers are trained.

Dosage

Dosage is typically assessed in terms of the number of specific 'units' (e.g. lessons) of an intervention that have been delivered (Domitrovich et al., 2008). It is simple to quantify and therefore among the most widely assessed aspects of implementation. Indeed, around half of all studies that have examined implementation in this field have included measures of dosage (Durlak and DuPre, 2008). The theoretical rationale for examining dosage extends the inoculation metaphor introduced in Chapter 1, suggesting that a certain amount of exposure is required in order for children to reap the benefits of a given SEL intervention, in much the same way that certain drugs need to build up in the body before they become effective in fighting infection or disease. So, for example, fluoxetine (Prozac) can take up to six weeks to produce clinical effects.

Research suggests a general trend towards a positive dose–response relationship. That is, schools/classes which deliver the required number of lessons achieve better outcomes than those which do not. For example, Rosenblatt and Elias (2008) found that the *Talking with TJ* SEL intervention was more successful in preventing achievement loss in students transitioning from elementary to middle/high school in classes where higher dosages of the intervention were delivered than those where lower dosages were delivered. However, Domitrovich et al. (2010a) cite several studies where no such relationship was found. These authors raise methodological questions that have been asked in relation to other aspects of implementation, noting in particular the schism between self-report and independent observation (see above). This factor which may be particularly pertinent for dosage, where self-ratings may be inflated because of social desirability effects.

Aside from the aforementioned mixed research findings, there are other dosage-related issues that make this aspect of implementation (and its influence on outcomes) somewhat more complicated than it may at first seem. Firstly, a dosage model may be difficult to develop for certain types of SEL programmes, for example those in which a structured, taught curriculum is not a central or mandatory component (e.g. the Caring School Community programme in the USA and the secondary SEAL programme in England – see Chapter 4). Furthermore, examining dosage in simplistic, quantitative terms potentially misses (or at least, underplays) the variation in pacing that teachers may implement based on their judgement of whether key concepts have been internalised by students, generalised to other settings, and so on. Relatively lower dosage may not therefore necessarily be indicative of poor implementation, but rather that a given teacher has spent more time to carefully ensure that students in his/her class have understood what is being taught before moving on. Finally, research in the field has typically analysed dosage in binary terms (e.g. high versus low dosage), which assumes a threshold model underpins the dose-response relationship for SEL. A more nuanced approach would be the use of dose-response curves, which would allow clarification of whether such a threshold exists (e.g. a dosage 'hinge point' after which outcomes improve dramatically). Such an approach would also allow for the testing of alternative models, such as a linear (e.g. response increases incrementally in line with increased dosage) or curvilinear (e.g. response increases incrementally in line with increased dosage up to a 'saturation' point, after which no additional benefits are seen) relationship.

Quality

How might we define 'quality' in terms of SEL implementation? There is perhaps an immediate danger of overlap and circularity with other elements such as fidelity (see above). If fidelity brings better outcomes, 'implementation with fidelity' may become synonymous with 'high quality implementation' (see Domitrovich and Greenberg, 2000). In the interests of clarity, and to draw a clearer demarcation between quality and other elements of implementation, it may be useful to think of it in terms of how well the content of a given SEL is taught by a given teacher. We might call this the 'delivery behaviour' (Domitrovich et al., 2010a). In these terms, we can think of 'implementation quality' as being similar to 'teaching quality', and therefore encompassing the pedagogical methods used, the extent to which lesson objectives were covered successfully, the teacher's interpersonal style and level of enthusiasm, and the provision of opportunities to generalise skills taught to other contexts. Although it makes intuitive sense that each of these aspects of quality would influence the success of the intervention being implemented, the research base is rather limited. For example, Durlak and DuPre's (2008) review found that only around 10 per cent of studies assessed quality, perhaps because examining them would necessitate time-consuming and costly observations (Domitrovich et al., 2010a). Where research has been conducted, it has produced mixed results. For example, while Kam et al. (2003) found no overall relationship between implementation quality (operationalised by observer ratings of how well teachers taught lesson concepts and skills and the extent to which these were generalised across the school day) and student outcomes in their study of the PATHS curriculum, they *did* find that quality interacted with leadership support (see section on 'factors affecting implementation' below) to predict outcomes. That is, schools where there was high-quality implementation *and* strong leadership support produced better outcomes.

Participant responsiveness

How do children and young people – the 'target audience' of SEL – receive and respond to a given intervention as it is delivered? Greenberg et al. (2005) suggest that we might look to the extent to which participants express liking for it, actively engage in activities and acknowledge its benefits as good indicators, since such behaviours are likely to be correlated with acceptance and more beneficial outcomes. Durlak and DuPre (2008) provide a similar definition, noting the importance of the extent to which a programme stimulates the interest or holds the attention of participants.

The responsiveness of participants is likely to be strongly influenced by other aspects of implementation and the various factors affecting it. In terms of the former, implementation quality (see above) is an obvious candidate. A teacher who delivers lessons with enthusiasm and uses methods that are engaging and participatory is much more likely to elicit positive responses among his or her class. In terms of the latter, the characteristics of the programme itself – in particular the age-appropriateness of materials and suggested teaching methods – are crucial. For example, many popular SEL programmes utilise puppets and other creative teaching aids in the materials for young children precisely because these are known to capture their attention and support their learning (Crepeau and Richards, 2003).

Programme reach

Consideration of programme reach may seem somewhat moot given the universalist model embodied within SEL. Surely the point is that SEL programmes reach all children and young people? However, even when a universal approach is taken, the rate of participation among children and young people may vary, either as a function of individual differences (e.g. children missing school or being withdrawn for other work) or school practices (e.g. a programme only being delivered to a specific class or year group). For example, in our evaluation of the secondary SEAL in England, we found significant variation in the extent to which our participants reported that they and other pupils had been involved in the programme. This rate of involvement also changed over time (Humphrey et al., 2010).

What does the research tell us about the importance of programme reach? Well, the first thing to say is that only a handful of studies have actually examined it. For example, only five of the studies reviewed by Durlak and DuPre (2008) collected data on programme reach, none of which were evaluating universal SEL interventions. However, the data from these evaluations can still provide an indication of the importance of this aspect of implementation. In their effectiveness trial of the Early Risers programme (an intervention that provides targeted support for children demonstrating early aggressive behaviour), August et al. (2006) found that the participation rate influenced intervention outcomes.

Programme differentiation and monitoring of control groups

I have conflated these two factors as they are both essentially about the 'usual practice' of schools prior to the adoption and implementation of an SEL programme. In schools that take on an intervention, the extent to which intervention activities can be distinguished from existing practice (programme differentiation) provides vital information that can help us to understand what has led to any change in outcomes (or lack thereof) (Dusenbury et al., 2003). Such information can also be useful in developing knowledge about how a school's SEL foundations affect the success of an adopted intervention. On the one hand, high levels of programme differentiation ('revolution') may be desirable because a given intervention is then seen as more distinctive. It may therefore be more likely to 'add unique value' to current practice. On the other hand, low levels of programme differentiation ('evolution') may be advantageous because the intervention will feel more 'familiar' to staff and presumably be easier to assimilate within existing processes and practices. Unfortunately, research that tests these competing hypotheses is currently lacking.

In terms of the monitoring of control groups, knowing the practices to which a given intervention is being compared is vital. For example, if the intervention fails to produce better outcomes than those reported in control schools, this may not be a failure of the intervention itself, but rather that those comparator schools were involved in implementing other, possibly similar unspecified activities and interventions that confounded the comparison. Recent research, such as a study by the Social and Character Development Research Consortium (2010), provides a useful example. This particular study, which involved a large, multi-site randomised controlled trial (RCT) evaluation of seven SEL interventions, attempted to develop and use a standard measure of 'social and character development activities' that could be used for the purposes of assessing both programme differentiation and monitoring of control schools. A key initial finding was that in the control schools, more than half of teachers and up to 90 per cent of school leaders reported engaging in a variety of classroom and school-wide activities designed explicitly to promote SEL. This reinforces the view that most schools – even those that have not adopted a 'named' intervention – are likely to be addressing SEL. This fundamentally changes the way we should consider outcomes of SEL evaluations because control groups must be thought of as 'usual practice' rather than 'no treatment'.

Factors affecting implementation

Each of the different aspects of implementation discussed above has been shown (some more consistently than others) to influence the outcomes of SEL and related interventions. The same body of research also tells us that there is considerable variation in them – that is, school staff implement SEL programmes with different levels of fidelity, dosage, quality and so on. A key question then is, 'where does this variation in implementation come from?' Knowing the answer(s) to this question has enormous practical implications. If we know what factors influence implementation variability, then we can build a model for the optimal conditions for effective implementation that can be communicated to schools as part of the programme dissemination process. Fortunately, a great deal is already known about these factors, thanks to the work of authors such as Durlak and DuPre (2008), Forman et al. (2009) and Greenberg et al. (2005), whose review work is synthesised in Table 6.2.

Available space does not permit a detailed analysis of each of the myriad factors in Table 6.2, so I conflate some and devote the most discussion to those that are generally considered to be more influential than others.

Preplanning and foundations

The preplanning and foundations in place prior to the adoption of a given SEL intervention provide the bedrock for later success (or failure!) in implementation. Greenberg et al. (2005) outline a range of important factors that each focus on a different aspect of the change process, which we might pose as questions to be asked of a school. Is there a *need* for change? Is the school *ready* for change? Does the school have the *capacity* to effect change? Are staff *aware* of the need for change? Is there a *commitment and engagement* in the change process? Is there any *incentive* for change? Finally, is there a *history of successful change* in the school?

Beyond these crucial factors, we might also look at the extent to which there is a shared vision for the intervention within the school. What do staff (and students) understand about the nature of the intervention? What are their expectations in terms of what outcomes the programme will influence and the amount of change that can be expected in these outcomes? What amount and type of input on their part do they believe is required in order to achieve said changes? In our evaluation of the secondary SEAL programme in England, we

Table 6.2 Factors affecting implementation of SEL interventions

Domain/level	General descriptor	Durlak and DuPre (2008)	Greenberg et al. (2005)	Forman et al. (2009)
Preplanning and foundations	Awareness		√ 'awareness'	
	Buy-in	√ 'shared vision'	√ 'commitment and engagement'	√ 'alignment with school philosophy'
	Staff involvement	√ 'formulation of tasks'		√ 'engaging the school in planning'
	Incentive to change	√ 'openness to change'	√ 'incentive for change'	
Implementation support system	Provision of training	√ 'training and technical assistance'	√ 'structure and content of training'	√ 'provision of high-quality training'
	Ongoing external support		√ 'timing of training'	
Implementation environment	Leadership support	√ 'leadership'	√ 'staff feel unsupported'	√ 'principal support'
	Integration with other aspects of school or curriculum	√ 'integration of new programming'		√ 'integrating the intervention with other school programmes or the curriculum'
	Time constraints	√ 'organisational capacity'	√ 'insufficient time'	
	Resource allocation		√ 'resources'	√ 'development of resources to sustain practice'
	Openness to change	√ 'openness to change'	√ 'incentive for change'	
	Competing priorities			
	Climate and relationships	√ 'positive work climate'	√ 'school and classroom climate'	
Implementer factors	Implementer experience, skills and confidence in delivery	√ 'self-efficacy and skill proficiency'	√ 'implementer skills and knowledge'	√ 'teacher characteristics and behaviours'
	Attitudes to SEL	√ 'perceived need for innovation'	√ 'implementer perceptions'	√ 'development of teacher support'
Programme characteristics	Quality of materials	√ 'characteristics of the innovation'	√ 'quality of materials'	
	Level of materials			
	Flexibility			

Adapted from Durlak and DuPre (2008), Greenberg et al. (2005) and Forman et al. (2009).

found high levels of variation in the answers given to such questions proffered by school staff, and this contributed to later implementation difficulties (Humphrey et al., 2010).

Research supports the idea that the foundations on which an SEL intervention is built have an effect on implementation quality. For example, Gottfredson and Gottfredson's (2002) scoping study of school-based prevention programmes (including SEL) in the United States demonstrated that factors such as a school's amenability to programme implementation were correlated with reported best practices in terms of the methods, content, level of use by school staff and other quality indicators.

Implementation support system

As with any educational innovation, school staff require initial training in order to acquire (or develop further) the necessary knowledge and skills to begin delivering SEL. Training also enables trainers to attend to psychological factors among implementers, such as expectations, motivation and sense of efficacy (Durlak and DuPre, 2008). In sum, it is seen as a crucial step in the facilitation of effective implementation (Dusenbury et al., 2003). The training models used vary from programme to programme in terms of duration (for example, total number of days required), timing and sequencing (for example, all training delivered at the outset or staggered over the period of initial implementation), teaching methods (for example, modelling and role plays, cascading) and mode of delivery (for example, face-to-face workshops or Internet-based training) (Greenberg et al., 2005). Given this variability and the overall importance ascribed to initial training, it is perhaps surprising how relatively little research has been conducted to examine its influence: 'There is little known about how training or staff development actually impacts teacher performance or student outcome' (Dusenbury et al., 2003: 249). However, a recent study of the RULER programme in the USA (Reyes et al., 2012) has provided some important insights. This research, which examined the influence of various aspects of implementation and associated factors (including training, dosage and quality) found no main effects of any factor alone on student outcomes. However, the authors did report several key interactions between factors. So, for example, moderate and high-quality implementers who attended more training sessions had students who achieved significantly higher scores in emotional literacy.

Following initial training, many SEL programmes also utilise ongoing support, often referred to as 'coaching'. Ongoing support consists of a range of activities, which may include further training (or training of new staff), monitoring of implementation and feedback, modelling of lessons, providing emotional support, troubleshooting and so on. As with initial training, it also serves to facilitate implementers' motivation and commitment (Durlak and DuPre, 2008). Although there is not a great deal of research that has clearly documented the influence of ongoing support on implementation (Greenberg et al., 2005), that which has been published has indicated the powerful role that it can play. For example, Joyce and Showers' (2002) review of teacher professional development reported that when training was supplemented with ongoing support, 95 per cent of teachers applied the knowledge and skills they had developed in the classroom, compared to only 5 per cent for those given initial training alone. Similarly, Dufrene et al. (2005) reported that implementation monitoring and provision of feedback and retraining dramatically increased fidelity of implementation (albeit with students in a peer tutoring intervention rather than adult SEL implementers).

Given the above, the provision of ongoing support for schools may also help to explain the increased variability in implementation that is often observed when SEL programmes are 'brought to scale' (that is disseminated and implemented beyond the environs of an efficacy trial) (Elias et al., 2003). As noted elsewhere, recent reviews have observed that when programmes are implemented in real-world settings, schools are much less likely to access the types of resources, support and technical assistance typically afforded in research trials (Shucksmith, 2007). This may be for a variety of reasons, from financial considerations (ongoing support is usually provided gratis in research trials but in real-world settings may incur additional costs that schools are not willing or able to pay) to the basic issue of availability (there may simply not be sufficiently qualified/experienced coaches within geographical reach of a school or schools adopting a proven intervention).

Implementation environment

Leadership support

It has become something of a truism that the support provided by school leadership for *any* educational innovation or initiative is a crucial factor in determining whether it 'takes hold'. As Leithwood et al. (2008) state, 'Leadership acts as a catalyst without which other good things are unlikely to happen' (p. 28). I would argue that this is particularly true of SEL interventions, which can be met with resistance and scepticism among staff in the way that more traditional, academically focused initiatives are not. In my experience, this is particularly true in secondary/high schools. School leadership support can influence SEL implementation in many ways, for example in setting school priorities, setting a clear vision, securing funding and other important resources, allocating time for training, and so on (Durlak and DuPre, 2008). A useful case example is seen in a study by Kam et al. (2003). As noted elsewhere, this effectiveness research on the impact of the PATHS curriculum found null results when compared to usual practice. However, when the authors mined their implementation data from the PATHS schools, they found significant variation between schools in terms of leadership support. When this was modelled against outcome data, significantly greater reductions in aggression and behavioural dysregulation were evident for students in PATHS schools with higher degrees of leadership support. Furthermore, the aforementioned school-based prevention survey by Gottfredson and Gottfredson (2002) found leadership support to be one of the strongest correlates of a variety of implementation quality indicators.

Resources and priorities

Alongside the crucial catalytic push given by strong leadership, the resources available to support SEL implementation are critical. As Raudenbush (2008) notes, 'Resources play a prominent role . . . by facilitating the enactment of proven instructional regimes' (p. 207). Greenberg et al. (2005) agree, citing the importance of human, informational, technological, financial and physical resources as key components necessary for programme implementation. Finally, Elias et al. (2003) state that 'the effective use of economic and social capital often underlies the ultimate success of real change' (p. 312). I have conflated discussion of this factor with priorities based on the assumption that if SEL is considered a priority, the crucial resources noted above are more likely to be allocated. Of course, the reverse would also be true in a school where SEL is not considered vital or important.

Unresolved problems with resource allocation and time constraints can pervade every aspect of the implementation process, contributing to eventual implementation failure in extreme cases. A case example can be seen in the secondary SEAL programme in England. Schools implementing SEAL received little or no additional financial funding to aid their implementation, meaning that other resources – in particular human resources – had to be allocated from within existing systems. Hence it was viewed by many staff as an additional task in an already busy and highly pressured working context. In this set of circumstances, a feeling of lack of available time is understandable, and staff dealt with this by prioritising their tasks. It was at this stage in the process that SEAL began to drift, unable to compete in the minds of staff with delivery of the academic curriculum. When Smith et al. (2007) questioned schools about their decrease in implementation activity in the secondary SEAL pilot, they found that 'many staff said that the pilot had not been a priority due to their involvement in other programmes of work and initiatives combined with the pressures of delivering their core curriculum and teaching and learning responsibilities' (p. 44). Forman et al.'s (2009) research on the implementation experience of teachers in the USA shows that such issues are likely to be universal. One quote in particular is striking in its resonance: 'I can't take the time out to teach these lessons, because if they [students] don't do well on their reading and math, we'll lose our jobs' (Forman et al., 2009: 32).

Implementer factors

With such a strong focus on SEL intervention features and their implementation alongside general contextual features that are known to be important, it can be easy to overlook the implementers themselves – who are typically classroom teachers (Forman et al., 2009). Research has shown that what each implementer 'brings to the table' can be vital in determining how they implement a given programme. As a starting point, Greenberg et al. (2005) make the salient observation that since general pedagogic and interpersonal competencies span areas of instruction, teachers who are effective in teaching academic subjects can also be successful SEL implementers. However, there is significant variation in the level of awareness, knowledge and understanding of SEL among members of the teaching community, and indeed levels of comfort in delivering instruction in this area. There can be resistance, for example, among teachers who feel that SEL is not part of their remit as educators (Humphrey et al., 2010).

〰️ **Points for Reflection**

- Why do some teachers feel that SEL is not their responsibility?

The teacher's own levels of social and emotional competence may also be a determining factor in their approach to implementation. Jennings and Greenberg's (2009) review suggests that teachers who have high levels of social awareness, exhibit pro-social values and are effective in managing their emotions and relationships with others are more adequately primed to implement SEL effectively because these competencies facilitate better relationships with their students, contribute to a more positive classroom climate and help them deal with stress in adaptive ways. Our qualitative research on the implementation of the primary SEAL small-group work initiative in England supports this assertion. In this study, a variety of stakeholders consistently noted the importance of implementers' social and emotional skills as being central to their effectiveness (Humphrey et al., 2008; Humphrey et al., 2009).

However, skill alone is only part of the picture. Teachers' attitudes toward SEL are also vitally important, affecting their practice in powerful ways. Recent research on this topic suggests that these attitudes should essentially be thought of in three dimensions (Brackett et al., 2012). The first of these is *comfort* – do teachers feel they have the ability to deliver effective SEL in the classroom? The second is *commitment* to SEL – that is, are they willing to engage in ongoing professional development in this area? The final aspect is *culture*. This taps a teacher's perceptions of whether the general ethos of the school in which they work is supportive of practices related to SEL – including the level of support and commitment from their leadership (see above). Brackett et al. (2012) propose that teachers whose comfort and commitment to SEL is low, and who perceive that their school culture is incongruent with it, will be less likely to deliver programmes effectively.

Hence, both the 'will' and 'skill' of teachers are important factors that influence their implementation behaviour. The former, whether taking the form of scything scepticism or unconditional acceptance, will be underpinned by attitudes, values and beliefs that are likely to be deeply entrenched and hence difficult to shift. The latter is more amenable to change, but given this it is perhaps surprising how few SEL programmes explicitly address the issue through training (Jennings and Greenberg, 2009). Notable exceptions include the SEAL programme (Department for Education and Skills, 2005a) and the Emotionally Intelligent Classroom approach (Brackett, 2006).

Finally, the psychological experiences of teachers can also directly influence aspects of implementation. A recent implementation study of the PATHS curriculum by Ransford et al. (2009) demonstrated how levels of stress experienced, feelings of burnout and perceived efficacy each contributed to factors such as dosage and quality. Hence, just as we must consider the differences between school contexts (for example, leadership support), we must also consider individual differences between implementers. However, not all research supports the idea that teacher characteristics have a clear bearing on implementation. In their study of the Head Start REDI (Research-based, Developmentally Informed) programme, Domitrovich et al. (2009) found a range of professional characteristics to be unrelated to changes in implementation fidelity beyond chance levels.

Programme characteristics

As seen in previous chapters, there is a great deal of heterogeneity in the myriad SEL programmes that are implemented by schools. Recall that in Chapter 1 we explored the three broad dimensions by which we can classify different approaches – reach (e.g. universal versus targeted), flexibility (e.g. prescriptive versus flexible) and component structure (e.g. single component versus multi-component). In addition, we might look to the content, quality and format of materials (Greenberg et al., 2005). Are they age-appropriate and developmentally sequenced, for example? Are manuals and associated guidance documents user-friendly, and presented in a clear, logical sequence that will facilitate effective high-quality implementation among staff? Graczyk et al. (2000) suggest that the most effective teacher manuals are those that include a comprehensive 'scope and sequence' chart, provide information on programme theory and how this influences design and delivery, clearly outline the objectives of the intervention and include detailed lesson plans.

For a useful example of how the characteristics of SEL programmes can influence their implementation, let us return to the meta-analyses noted earlier that found no advantage to multi-component approaches when compared to those with a single component (Durlak et al., 2011; Wilson and Lipsey, 2007). The explanation for this somewhat unexpected finding may be found in how the component structures of programmes influence implementation. We know that more complex, multi-component interventions requiring action at multiple levels and the commitment of multiple participants take longer to implement successfully (Durlak and DuPre, 2008), are more likely to be discontinued (Yeaton and Sechrest, 1981) and typically become diluted due to their broader scope (Wilson and Lipsey, 2007). Such issues may mean that while multi-component programmes *should* produce better outcomes than those with only a single component, the increased implementation difficulties associated with the former reduces their effectiveness.

A further, related aspect of the characteristics of a given programme that is likely to affect implementation is the extent to which it is ready to be delivered 'off the shelf'. Here we might consider the completeness of the programme materials, resources and associated guidance. As we have already seen, competing priorities often mean that the amount of time available for staff to be able to prepare and deliver SEL content may be limited. In this context, programmes that lack clear guidance or whose materials and resources are incomplete will be more difficult to implement successfully. This was a particularly pertinent issue in our evaluations of the SEAL programme in England. In our secondary SEAL evaluation, the lack of clear, directional guidance was a clear barrier to effective implementation (Humphrey et al., 2010; Lendrum et al., 2012). By contrast, the primary SEAL small-group work component (which, it should be noted, is a targeted rather than universal SEL intervention) had a clear, fairly prescriptive manual to guide implementation, but key content was missing from the intervention. For example, at the time of our study, there were only lesson materials available for four of the seven themed interventions. This meant that staff whose pupils were in need of one of the other three interventions had to develop materials themselves (Humphrey et al., 2008).

Points for Reflection

- How might research findings on the different aspects of implementation and the factors that influence them be used to refine programmes and improve future practice?

Bringing it all together – the implementation quality framework

Understanding the implementation process is vital. It gives us insights into how and why an SEL intervention works and as such is a crucial element of developing knowledge about how best to secure positive outcomes for children and young people. Although there are gaps and inconsistencies in the research base, it is clear that 'implementation matters' (Durlak and DuPre, 2008). How then, may we use the knowledge base in this area to good effect? As with other aspects of SEL, we need an 'organising idea'.

Domitrovich et al.'s (2008) multi-level conceptual framework for enhancing implementation quality (IQ) is very useful in this regard. They position the IQ of a given intervention as part of an ecological system with influences at different levels:

- The *macro-level* includes such factors as community influences, government policies, leadership and human capital.

- The *school-level* includes features such as the culture and climate of the school, its characteristics (e.g. size), the resources available and the expertise of staff.

- The *individual-level* includes the 'will and skill' of individual staff, in addition to their psychological characteristics.

The intervention model itself varies in terms of:

- *core elements* – which are akin to the 'critical components' referred to earlier in this chapter;

- *standardisation* – which refers to the extent to which intervention practices and procedures vary across different sites and contexts;

- *delivery model* – which includes the mode, frequency, duration and timing of the intervention.

The intervention is underpinned by a support system to which the same elements may be applied:

- *core elements* – which may refer to initial and ongoing training, and coaching or mentoring;

- *standardisation* – which becomes particularly important when demand for a given intervention grows and programme developers begin to adopt a 'train the trainer' model;

- *delivery model* – which considers how training and support are provided (e.g. live versus video training, intensive versus brief training).

Domitrovich et al. (2008) propose that attention to each of these various components and levels is vital in enhancing IQ. However, they also use the model to highlight the need for theory-driven research in which adaptations and modifications at each level/component are systematically monitored to determine their effect on IQ and outcomes. They state that at present 'there are more questions than answers about how to integrate preventive interventions in schools so that they are implemented with high quality and sustained over time' (p. 21).

Further Reading

Domitrovich, C. et al. (2008) 'Maximising the implementation quality of evidence-based preventive interventions in schools: a conceptual framework', *Advances in School Mental Health Promotion*, 1: 6–28.

Durlak, J. and DuPre, E. (2008) 'Implementation matters: a review of the research on the influence of implementation on program outcomes and the factors affecting implementation', *American Journal of Community Psychology*, 41: 327–50.

7

Outcomes of SEL

Overview

The aim of this chapter is to examine the extent to which universal SEL interventions affect a range of outcomes for children and young people. Particular attention is given to the evidence pertaining to changes in academic progress. The chapter continues by outlining and discussing a range of issues that affect our interpretation of SEL outcome research, including the role of programme developers in evaluation, confirmation bias and adverse effects, efficacy versus effectiveness, and the basic question of what constitutes a good outcome in a universal intervention. The chapter concludes by considering examples of SEL outcome research that have 'gone against the grain' and exploring what may be learned from them.

Key Points

- The evidence base suggests that high-quality universal SEL interventions can be effective in promoting a range of outcomes for children and young people.
- The task of determining the nature, extent and significance of the impact of SEL on academic performance is confounded by factors such as the explicit academic content of some programmes.

- There are a range of issues that suggest caution is required in interpreting SEL outcome research, including methodological limitations of studies and problems with transferability of findings.
- The overall picture emerging from the field is arguably skewed by factors such as confirmation bias and a predominance of efficacy (as opposed to effectiveness) trials.
- SEL evaluations that yield 'null results' can provide insights that aid the development of the field.

What does the research tell us about the impact of SEL on outcomes for children and young people?

The journey to this point of the book has taken us through such issues as the meaning and history of SEL, its place in education systems across the world, how it is assessed and how it is implemented. Ultimately though, the subject matter of this penultimate chapter is what has proven to be at once the key allure of SEL and perhaps the source of most controversy surrounding the field. Education systems across the world have become increasingly focused on the notion of 'testable' outcomes in the last several decades. This is particularly true of SEL, which as already noted can be viewed with scepticism among some educators. Hence, it is not enough to believe that promoting SEL in school is 'the right thing to do'. In the contemporary educational climate, it has to be proven to improve measurable outcomes for children and young people.

So what does the research tell us? Overall, the evidence base pertaining to the effect of universal SEL interventions on outcomes is positive, if not unequivocal. The meta-analysis by Durlak et al. (2011) demonstrated:

- moderate effects on:
  - social and emotional skills, with an average effect size of 0.57 (equivalent to a 22 percentile-point improvement as a result of participation in an SEL programme);

- small effects on:
  - attitudes (average effect size = 0.23, a 9 percentile-point improvement);

- positive social behaviour (average effect size = 0.24, a 9 percentile-point improvement);
- conduct problems (average effect size = 0.22, a 9 percentile-point improvement);
- emotional distress (average effect size = 0.24, a 9 percentile-point improvement);
- academic performance (average effect size = 0.27, an 11 percentile-point improvement).

Wilson and Lipsey's (2007) meta-analysis is also pertinent here, although they had a more specific remit (school-based interventions with a focus on aggressive and disruptive behaviour). The authors found similar results to Durlak and colleagues. For example, they found an average effect size of 0.21 of universal programmes on children's behaviour problems. A number of reviews in relevant areas (e.g. Adi et al., 2007; Blank et al., 2009; Weare and Nind, 2011) have also yielded largely positive findings. However, the 'vote-counting' approaches to reporting in such studies (where statistical significance is used to create a simplistic dichotomy between 'significant' and 'null' studies) places them lower in the evidence hierarchy than the aforementioned meta-analyses (Durlak, 1991). In addition to the fact that overall findings are positive, they are also broadly in line with the predictions one might make from the SEL logic model (CASEL, 2007). So, for example, larger gains are seen in proximal (e.g. social and emotional skills) variables than in distal (e.g. academic performance) variables.

 Points for Reflection

- Which of the above outcomes are likely to be the most influential in determining the widespread adoption of evidence-based approaches to SEL and why?

Limitations and gaps in the evidence base

However, there are also a number of issues that suggest that caution is required. Firstly, despite the fact that SEL is clearly an international phenomenon in terms of policy and practice, the vast majority of the evidence base is derived solely from the United States. Indeed, around 90 per cent of the studies included in both of the major meta-analyses noted above were located there. 'Transferability' cannot be assumed (Weare and Nind, 2011), particularly given the cultural differences evident in the emotional domain (see Chapter 2) and the variation in the role played by government policy, the composition of SEL and its function in countries across the world (see Chapter 3). It is encouraging to note that evidence has begun to emerge outside the US. These have involved field-tests of cultural adaptations of existing programmes (e.g. Malti et al.'s (2011) evaluation of the PATHS curriculum in Switzerland) and home-grown interventions (e.g. Kimber et al.'s (2008) trial of the SET programme in Sweden). However, there is clearly still an urgent need for the development of the non-US SEL research base.

There are also a variety of methodological limitations in the body of evidence pertaining to the outcomes of SEL. These span the key areas outlined earlier in this book, including monitoring and assessment and implementation. So, for example, in Durlak et al.'s (2011) review:

- 53 per cent of studies relied solely on child self-report, raising issues of reliability in studies involving younger children, and for some evaluations questions over whether changes in outcomes actually translated into real-life behavioural expression (given the discrepancy between typical and maximal behaviour discussed in Chapter 5);

- 42 per cent did not monitor implementation in any way, meaning what school staff actually did, and in particular how closely they stuck to intervention guidelines, was unknown. This creates a 'black box' problem in which the change mechanisms underpinning outcomes cannot be verified;

- 19 per cent were unpublished reports and therefore not subjected to academic scrutiny (although there are very sound reasons for including these, not least to balance out the bias towards publication of statistically significant outcomes – Durlak, 1991);

- 24 per cent used measures with poor or no reported reliability, meaning that they may not tap consistent responses over time;

- 49 per cent used measures with poor or no reported validity, meaning that they may not measure what they purport to measure.

There are also a number of gaps in the evidence base that limit our ability to make definitive statements about the effectiveness of universal school-based SEL interventions. Most notably, we still know comparatively little about:

- How different programme components interact with one another to produce effects on outcomes. As already discussed, we know from the two major meta-analyses that multi-component interventions may be no more effective than single-component programmes. However, beyond this basic distinction, we know little about how different combinations of the core components of SEL interventions introduced in Chapter 1 (e.g. curriculum, environment/ethos, parents/community) influence outcomes.

- How universal and indicated/targeted interventions interact with one another. Despite the intuitive logic of a staged approach, there is remarkably little evidence that directly tests for differential effects of universal, targeted/indicated and universal *plus* targeted/indicated provision on outcomes. Exceptions to this are the study by Sheffield et al. (2006) discussed later in this chapter, and the trial of the 'PATHS to PAX' programme (Domitrovich et al., 2010b), which has yet to report outcomes at the time of writing.

- SEL interventions for those in secondary/high school, which make up only 13 per cent of the evidence base (Durlak et al., 2011). This is perhaps understandable given the general emphasis on early intervention throughout education and related fields. However, attention to this area is of crucial importance given the increased prevalence of mental health disorders in adolescence when compared to childhood (Green et al., 2005) and the substantial differences between primary/elementary and secondary/high schools in terms of increased size, greater emphasis on ability and competition, and reduced quality of relationships with teachers in the latter (Humphrey and Ainscow, 2006).

The 'bottom line' in education – academic performance

There is a valid argument that improvement of proximal variables such as social and emotional skills and positive social behaviour should constitute a good reason for investment in SEL in and of itself. However, the pressures placed on schools to raise academic standards through centralised policy drives (see, for example, the No Child Left Behind Act in the US) mean that schools typically make decisions regarding programme adoption based on the notion that SEL will ultimately improve children's academic scores. This issue was duly noted by Zins et al. (2004): 'Receptivity for SEL programming will be even greater if a strong empirical case is made connecting the enhancement of social and emotional influences to improved school behaviour and academic performance' (p. 5). This has, of course, been noted in the SEL community and programme developers are keen to emphasise the academic credentials of their interventions. Indeed, several SEL programmes have been revised to accommodate a more explicit academic orientation in recent years. For example, the most recent edition of the Second Step materials incorporates activities and resources designed to boost executive/cognitive skills such as focusing attention and using memory. Likewise, the UK version of the PATHS curriculum contains a series of lessons on study skills with similar, academically oriented content. This is welcome and in line with calls by CASEL and others to infuse programmes with academic skill building, but it also means that the parameters of what SEL actually constitutes (see Chapter 2) are stretched even further.

What does the research tell us about the impact of SEL on academic performance? As before, Durlak et al. (2011) is our starting point. Their review identified 35 studies that had assessed academic performance as an outcome. As noted at the start of this chapter, the subsequent analysis indicated an average effect size of 0.27, equivalent to an 11 percentile-point increase as a result of a child having participated in an SEL programme. This particular finding has undoubtedly been the most widely celebrated of any from the meta-analysis. The authors themselves point out that the academic improvements brought about by SEL programming are 'comparable to the results . . . of strictly educational interventions' (Durlak et al., 2011: 416).

This set of findings has been accepted rather uncritically, but as before closer inspection reveals a picture that is rather more complex than SEL proponents would perhaps like to believe. Beginning with the effect size itself, the amount of change in children's academic scores brought about by SEL is actually somewhat *lower* than average when one considers the findings of John Hattie's (2009, 2012) seminal synthesis of 900 meta-analyses relating to academic achievement. Examining a bewildering range of around 150 different influences, he found an average effect size of 0.4. Hattie calls this the 'hinge point', at which 'the effects of innovation enhance achievement in such a way that we can notice real-world differences' (2009: 17). Viewed from this perspective, the impact of SEL is arguably less impressive. However, we must bear in mind that improvements in academic performance are a distal outcome in the logic model – proximal changes in social and emotional skills are arguably the central goal.

Another important issue for us to analyse is exactly *how* SEL impacts upon children's attainment. Recall that the logic model suggests that its influence is both direct and indirect (via its influence on attachment to school and risky behaviour) (see Chapter 2). A complicating factor in this equation is that several of the SEL programmes examined in the 35 studies analysed by Durlak and colleagues actually contain explicit academic components. For example, the Caring School Communities programme (previously known as the Child Development Project) outlined in Chapter 4 contains 'literature-based reading instruction' (Solomon et al., 2000: 7). Similarly, the Responsive Classroom approach 'is designed to emphasise social and academic learning equally' (Rimm-Kaufman et al., 2007: 404). Finally, in Cook et al.'s (1999) evaluation of the Comer School Development Project, 'achievement gains were found in schools with a more explicit academic focus' (p. 535). Such findings make it difficult to disentangle what proportion of SEL's influence on attainment is achieved through the pathways suggested in the logic model and what is actually the result of explicit academic instruction embedded in some programmes. As with other areas of focus in this chapter, further research is necessary.

Key issues in interpreting SEL outcome research

What constitutes a good outcome?

 Points for Reflection

- What constitutes a good outcome? How much change in a given variable is required to justify the input required to achieve that change?

This is such a basic question that it is rarely asked, but the answers are far from straightforward. Let us assume, for example, that we have an SEL evaluation study designed with a measurement protocol that has overcome the range of issues outlined in this chapter. The rigour of the overall design (for the sake of argument, it is a randomised trial using multi-informant, multi-source data) means that we can be very confident in the veracity of any results. In such a hypothetical context, what would we deem to be an outcome that is meaningful and justifies the effort expended in implementation? We certainly cannot rely upon statistical significance testing, affected so greatly as it is by sample size (meaning that large studies often produce effects that are unlikely to be due to chance but are nonetheless not meaningful on any practical level, and smaller studies might miss important changes because of reduced test sensitivity) (Cohen, 1993).

We might instead look at effect size analysis, which provides an estimate of the amount of change that has occurred in a given outcome measure, typically expressed in standardised units – but how much change is 'enough'? Cohen's (1992) indexes of effect size are often used as thresholds (with changes of 0.2, 0.5 and 0.8 standardised units considered to be small, medium and large, respectively), but they are arbitrary thresholds whose meaningfulness varies according to what is being measured. For example, we saw earlier that Hattie (2009) suggests that an effect size of 0.4 is the 'hinge point' for academic attainment. However, we also need to consider the target population and context of change. So, for example, we might ask what the normative expectations are for growth over time in a given variable/outcome, gaps in attainment of said outcome among particular groups, and the results from past research for similar programmes (Hill et al., 2008).

An additional problem is that effect size analysis tells us relatively little about the reliability of change or its importance in clinical terms (Jacobson and Truax, 1991). We might therefore ask two questions. First, does the amount of change observed exceed that which could be attributed to measurement error (reliable change)? Second, is the amount of change observed socially and/or clinically meaningful (clinically significant change) (Evans et al., 1998)? In relation to reliable change, there are formulae that can be applied that take into account the inherent internal consistency/reliability of the instrument to produce a threshold above which change can be considered reliable (see Evans et al., 1998). In relation to clinically significant change, it has been suggested that the fundamental principle is the extent to which individuals have moved from the 'dysfunctional population' range to the 'functional population' range on a given measure (Jacobson and Follette, 1984). This point raises another critical question though – for whom should we expect change? Greenberg (2010) states, 'in universal interventions, it is usually the case that a large percentage of the population begins without symptoms and thus it is unlikely (at least in the short term) that much of this population will change. In most cases, it is only in the higher symptom group of the population that larger effect sizes will be obtained' (p. 34).

This salient point is illustrated well in the national evaluation of the KidsMatter programme in Australia (Slee et al., 2009). This study reported small effect sizes for changes in children's mental health in participating schools, as measured by the Strengths and Difficulties

Questionnaire (Goodman, 1997). However, the authors' subsequent sub-group analyses demonstrated differential effects for children who scored in the normal, borderline and abnormal ranges of the SDQ at the study's baseline (e.g. no or small effects for those in the normal range, large effects for those in the abnormal range). Such effects are examined in more detail below (see 'Who benefits from SEL?').

The economics of SEL

A final consideration in determining what constitutes a good outcome for an SEL intervention – which is often neglected or even completely ignored – is the level of cost incurred (human, material, financial) in order to secure that outcome. This is where SEL research must enter the arena of economic evaluation.

In the current fiscal climate, in which education budgets are typically stretched, economic analyses of school-based interventions are crucial. It is not enough to simply know that a given SEL programme, if implemented well, will likely produce positive outcomes in specified domains. As noted in Chapter 6, the adoption and implementation of universal SEL interventions incurs certain costs (e.g. human, material, financial). It is of course vital that such costs do not outweigh the subsequent benefits in order for such interventions to be considered viable and sustainable. This is of particular concern at the level of educational policy:

> Just as business executives want to know how an investment would affect their company's bottom line, policymakers find it useful to ask not only whether government expenditures have the intended effects but also whether investing in child and adolescent program provides 'profits' to the children themselves, to taxpayers, and to society as a whole. (Duncan and Magnuson, 2007: 47)

In universal SEL programmes, the 'profit' referred to by Duncan and Magnuson may be in relation to economic growth associated with increased well-being and academic attainment or in savings made through successful prevention of maladaptive outcomes that would otherwise necessitate costly intervention (see Chapter 3).

Despite its obvious importance, the evidence base for economic analyses of universal SEL interventions currently lags far behind basic, outcomes-focused evaluations (Greenberg, 2010). Indeed, a recent systematic review conducted by McCabe (2008) revealed *no* published empirical studies in this area in relation to the primary phase of education, although an estimated analysis by the author using the PATHS curriculum as an example suggested that it would most likely prove to be cost-effective. Similarly, a review of interventions in secondary education by Hummel et al. (2009) revealed no published studies, but estimated analysis suggested a strong probability that some interventions would be cost-effective. However, a study commissioned by the Washington State Institute for Public Policy (Aos et al., 2004) on the costs and benefits of early intervention and prevention has provided some evidence pertaining directly to SEL. The authors examined a range of programme types (e.g. child welfare/ home visitation, mentoring, substance abuse prevention) among which were some well-known SEL interventions such as the Child Development Project/Caring School Community (see Chapter 4) and the Seattle Social Development Project (Hawkins et al., 1992), each of which yielded benefits that outweighed the costs per participant, in some cases to the tune of several thousand dollars. One of the key factors here appears to be the relatively low cost of universal SEL when compared to other approaches (for example, the Child Development Project was estimated to cost just $16 per child).

The role and influence of programme developers in SEL evaluation

An issue that has been given scant attention in SEL outcome research is who leads the evaluation itself. Most SEL evaluations to date have been led by programme developers (or individuals closely associated with programme developers). Indeed, Greenberg (2010) notes that in the broader field of prevention, few interventions have been independently replicated. This is an important issue because in other fields with a focus upon prevention and intervention (e.g. criminology, psychiatry), effect sizes have been shown to be considerably larger when programme developers are involved in evaluation studies (Eisner, 2009). For example, in a review of psychiatric interventions, studies where programme developers were directly involved in the study were nearly five times more likely to report positive results (Perlis et al., 2005). Similarly, in a meta-analysis of 300 studies of crime prevention interventions, Petrosino and Soydan (2005) found an average effect size of 0.47 for developer-led studies, contrasted to one of 0 for independent evaluations.

Criminologist Manuel Eisner (2009) offers two explanations for the startling differences in outcomes of these two types of study. The *cynical view* proposes that the more favourable results in developer-led trials stem from systematic biases that influence decision-making during a study. The *high fidelity view* argues that implementation of a given intervention is of a higher quality in studies in which the programme developer is involved, leading to better results. If the first view holds true, doubts may be cast over the SEL research base, dominated as it is by evaluations involving developers. If the second view holds true, then there is nothing inherently wrong with developer-led study results. However, as Eisner (2009) points out, their findings would still lack external validity because they could not be generalised to real-life settings. This issue is examined in more detail in the section on efficacy and effectiveness. To date, no analysis of developer-led/involved versus independent evaluations has been conducted on the SEL evidence base, but given the findings from such analyses in related fields and the implications for the notion of 'evidence-based practice', this should be a key priority for future research to address.

Confirmation bias and adverse effects

The current state of the SEL field is such that there is perhaps a risk of confirmation bias when researchers interpret outcomes in evaluation studies. Confirmation bias is the propensity for individuals to favour information that confirms their a priori beliefs. There is evidence of this phenomenon at work in both reviews and individual studies. For example, in Wells et al.'s (2003) systematic review of universal approaches to mental health promotion in schools, only two of 17 studies identified were of programmes taking a whole-school approach, one of which was described by as having limited generalisability because of methodological flaws and the programme only demonstrating moderately positive results. Despite this, the authors concluded 'the results of this review provide support for whole-school approaches' (Wells et al., 2003: 217).

In terms of individual studies, Cooke et al.'s (2007) single-group evaluation of Second Step in a city in Connecticut found expected improvements in a handful of student self-reported variables (such as consideration of others), but no improvement in others. There were no changes in directly observed student behaviours or disciplinary referrals. Somewhat worryingly, they also found significant increases in a range of negative outcomes, including negative coping, bullying and angry behaviour. These negative findings are not reported in the study abstract and are not addressed in the discussion section of the paper. The null results noted above are explained in a way that is consistent with the confirmation bias phenomenon – for example, the failure to find any changes in aggressive behaviour is framed as evidence of the programme having attenuated a rise in aggression among students.

Another example of SEL confirmation bias can be seen in Hallam et al.'s (2006) evaluation of the primary SEAL programme in England, which concluded that it had 'a major impact on children's well-being, confidence, social and communication skills, relationships, including bullying, playtime behaviour, pro-social behaviour and attitudes towards schools' (Hallam et al., 2006: 1). However, even the most rudimentary inspection of the research report itself demonstrates that the authors' conclusions are, at best, inaccurate (Craig, 2007). The assertion of the programme having a major impact on any of the areas specified above is simply not borne out by the data. Where there were statistically significant changes in measured outcomes, the associated effect sizes were marginal. However, the report also showed some potential adverse effects, including a decline in academic performance for younger children and negative changes in attitudes towards school and relationships with teachers among older children during the pilot (Humphrey, 2009). Furthermore, there were a number of key variables where SEAL made no difference whatsoever (e.g. attendance) (Craig, 2007).

As is evident above, the danger inherent in confirmation bias is that a skewed view of the benefits of SEL is presented, in which positive results are overstated and null results and/or potential adverse effects are effectively ignored. Weare and Nind (2011) highlight the importance of studying the latter as part of a comprehensive approach to determining 'what works' in the field. They note that we need to identify and distinguish between truly adverse effects and phenomena that simply represent greater reporting as a result of raised awareness brought about through a given intervention.

Efficacy versus effectiveness in SEL research

A further crucial dichotomy in research focusing on the outcomes of universal SEL interventions is that of efficacy versus effectiveness. *Efficacy* research refers to examining the effects of a given intervention under optimal, well-controlled conditions, whereas *effectiveness* research examines programme effects in 'real-world' conditions (Flay et al., 2005). Efficacy precedes effectiveness in the research process (Campbell, 2000; Flay et al., 2005). The SEL evidence base is primarily composed of research in the former at the expense of the latter. The potential dangers of such disparity were highlighted by Shucksmith and colleagues (2007):

> Studies . . . have seen the investment of massive sums of money in large multi-component longitudinal trials. The results that emerge from these are very useful and are showing the way towards the design of more effective interventions, yet there must be serious doubts as to the availability of such resources within normal education budgets. (p. 5)

These concerns, echoed by Greenberg et al. (2005), are well founded, because where research is conducted on SEL interventions in typical practice conditions, schools often fail to replicate reported intervention effects (e.g. Kam et al., 2003).

 Points for Reflection

- What reasons might underpin the failure of effectiveness trials to replicate effects observed in efficacy trials?

Furthermore, many of the claims made about the benefits of SEL are based on an evidence base that – because it is primarily composed of efficacy trials – lacks external validity. What is needed, therefore, is more of what Greenberg (2010) refers to as 'Type Two translational research', essentially effectiveness studies that examine the impact of efficacious interventions in uncontrolled settings. Given that we know that implementation becomes more variable in effectiveness settings, such studies should also pay close attention the factors that facilitate or impede quality implementation (Greenberg, 2010).

Who benefits from SEL? Student characteristics and differential outcomes

There is an assumption that the universalist model that is central to SEL yields universal gains. This is compounded by studies that treat children and young people as homogenous, typically reporting only average effects on outcomes (Adi et al., 2007). However, there is some evidence that this assumption is perhaps misplaced and that there are differential outcomes for sub-groups of students as a function of their characteristics. Much of the research thus far shows amplified effects for those exposed to varying levels of risk and adversity. Recall, for example, that the 'You Can Do It!' intervention in Australia only improved the literacy scores of children who were poorer readers to begin with (Ashdown and Bernard, 2011). In the same country, the evaluation of the KidsMatter initiative demonstrated positive effects only for children who began the study with clinically significant mental health difficulties (Slee et al., 2009). Finally, analysis of the benefits of the Second Step curriculum in Norway revealed much greater improvement in outcomes for students from low socio-economic backgrounds than for their more affluent peers (Holsen et al., 2009).

The above studies appear to demonstrate that the benefits of SEL vary as a function of participant characteristics, but further research is clearly needed in this area (Durlak et al., 2011). Indeed, Weisz et al. (2005) argue that understanding for whom and under what conditions interventions work is a compelling priority. As a general point, the failure to consistently examine these factors in detail seems somewhat out of sync with the preventive roots of SEL. That is, surely it would be sensible to examine the effects of what are ostensibly preventive interventions with specific groups of participants whose backgrounds suggest that they are more likely to experience negative outcomes? A useful exception is the study published by the Conduct Problems Prevention Research Group (1999), in which the effects of the Fast Track programme (which combined universal and targeted SEL) were examined separately for children deemed to be at an increased risk of maladaptive outcomes following initial screening. Such sub-group analyses should be a routine part of SEL outcome research.

This issue notwithstanding, the evidence that is available seems to indicate that SEL may not in fact be universally beneficial, but rather that its benefits could be limited to (or at least amplified greatly among) students who we may characterise as 'vulnerable' (e.g. those with existing emotional, behavioural or academic difficulties and/or those exposed to the effects of poverty or other risk factors). Indeed, this assertion is ratified by the findings of Wilson and Lipsey's (2007) meta-analysis. This is not a problem in and of itself, as it would still make SEL a very worthy enterprise indeed. But it does call into question the assertion that it is something we all need and can all benefit from. As noted in Chapter 3, this arguably generalises a risk model from some to all students.

Moderators of SEL outcomes – staying SAFE

As we saw in the previous chapter, there is a whole range of implementation factors that can moderate the outcomes of SEL interventions. In addition to these, it is important to consider whether a given programme exhibits the following four characteristics:

- **S**equenced – the application of a planned set of activities to develop skills sequentially in a step-by-step approach. This principle applies to both the general sequencing of implementation across different levels within the school (e.g. staff training, work with parents, policy development) and the more detailed sequencing of different activities within a skills-focused curriculum to ensure developmental appropriateness for pupils of different ages.

- **A**ctive – the use of active forms of learning such as role play. This applies equally to explicit opportunities for teaching and learning with students and training with staff. In either scenario, it is proposed that key social and emotional skills cannot be absorbed passively.

- **F**ocused – the devotion of sufficient time exclusively to the development of social and emotional skills. This means ensuring that the taught element of an intervention has its place in the school day, and that staff training and professional development time is planned and delivered regularly and consistently.

- **E**xplicit – the targeting of specific social and emotional skills. Changes in the school culture/environment alone are not sufficient to produce lasting change and there needs to be a strong curriculum-based element that provides pupils with explicit opportunities to develop skills such as empathy in a safe environment.

SEL programmes containing these 'SAFE' features were demonstrated to affect a wider range of outcomes and produce larger effects than those lacking them in both Durlak et al.'s (2011) meta-analysis of universal school-based SEL and in an earlier meta-analysis of after-school SEL programmes (Durlak et al., 2010). For example, the average effect size for social and emotional skills in SAFE programmes was 0.69 compared to 0.01 for non-SAFE programmes (Durlak et al., 2011). Interestingly, however, there was no such differential effect for academic performance.

Interpreting SEL evaluation studies with null results: a framework

The various issues noted above notwithstanding, it is fair to say that the majority of research in the field has pointed to the effectiveness of SEL programmes in improving a variety of important outcomes for children and young people. However, there are a number of SEL evaluation studies that have yielded 'null' results. That is, they found no benefit from SEL intervention when compared to usual practice. It is vital that such studies are given due consideration. Indeed, it is my contention that we have as much to learn from them as we do from those more widely celebrated studies where positive effects are noted. The insights that null studies can provide can lead to improvements in SEL theory, research and practice.

In this section I examine several case studies of null SEL evaluations and interpret each through a framework adapted from Raudenbush (2008). Raudenbush suggests two possible explanations for null results when an instructional regime is evaluated: theory failure and implementation failure. To this I add tentatively add a third: evaluation failure.

- *Theory failure* is evident when a programme has been implemented as designed and robustly evaluated, but there are problems with the underlying programme theory.

- *Implementation failure* occurs when a programme theory is sound and there has been a robust evaluation, but the intervention is not implemented as designed.

- *Evaluation failure* assumes a sound programme theory and implementation as planned, but posits that flaws in the research process lead to null results.

As we will see, each of these factors can work alone or in combination.

Case study 1: Secondary SEAL evaluation in England (Humphrey et al., 2010)

The secondary school element of the overall SEAL programme (which is described in detail in Chapter 4) was subject to a national evaluation by our research team at Manchester on behalf of the English government. In brief, our study consisted of a quasi-experimental pre-test/post-test control group design in which we tracked changes to key outcomes in a cohort of nearly 9,000 children attending 22 SEAL and 19 matched comparison schools over a two-year period. Alongside this, we also examined the process of implementation in nine of the 22 SEAL schools via longitudinal qualitative case studies. Analysis of our outcome data indicated that secondary SEAL had failed to impact upon the social and emotional skills, mental health difficulties, pro-social behaviour or behaviour problems of the children in our sample. The data from our case studies suggested that implementation of SEAL was extremely variable, fragmented and superficial within and between schools.

What light can our adapted framework shed on the findings of this study? In terms of theory failure, SEAL is closely aligned with Goleman's (1996) EI model, which as noted in earlier chapters has been the subject of considerable criticism. In terms of the theory of change underpinning SEAL, it was conceived as a loose enabling framework for school improvement rather than a prescriptive, manualised intervention that is more typical of universal SEL interventions (Weare, 2010). Our case study data suggested that while this more flexible approach was initially welcomed by staff in SEAL schools, ultimately it left them without a clear direction and focus in the implementation process. Indeed, this was perhaps the primary cause of the poor progress made. In this case, theory failure and subsequent implementation failure are inextricably linked. However, our more recent analyses of data from this study in which we modelled implementation against outcomes demonstrated that there was negligible or no effect from implementation quality. That is, schools classed as low/moderate/high quality in terms of SEAL implementation were barely distinguishable from one another in respect of student outcomes (Wigelsworth et al., 2012).

In terms of evaluation failure, the study relied on student self-report to assess outcomes, meaning that the null results could not be triangulated against another source(s) for verification purposes. Additionally, we were unable to randomly allocate schools to intervention and control groups. SEAL schools had already been chosen by their local authorities and we then recruited matched comparison schools. It is therefore important to consider the fact that there may have been latent differences between SEAL and control schools in our evaluation – such as motivation, interest in SEL and existing practices – which may have influenced our findings. Finally, some commentators argued that the 'bottom-up' nature of the secondary SEAL model precluded a traditional research design: 'Searching for overall conclusions about the impact of "being a SEAL school" is likely to lead us to a dead end' (Park, 2011).

Case Study 2: Social and Character Development Research Consortium multi-programme evaluation in the USA (SACDRC, 2010)

In this US-based study, a consortium of research teams conducted a multi-site randomised controlled trial involving seven universal SEL interventions (the Academic and Behavioural Competencies Program, the Competence support Program, Love in a Big World, Positive Action, PATHS, the 4Rs Program and Second Step) over a three-year period. A total of 74 elementary schools (containing a sample of over 6,000 children) across the seven study sites were randomly allocated to intervention and control groups. Outcome measurement focused on social and emotional competence, behaviour, academics and school climate, primarily through student self-report, but in some cases triangulated against teacher and/or parent informant-report surveys. Alongside this, the researchers monitored some aspects of implementation introduced in Chapter 6 – most notably, programme differentiation, control group monitoring and fidelity. They authors reported that the SEL programmes did not improve children's outcomes when considered together, individually or for specific sub-groups (e.g. those affected by poverty). Furthermore, they found no association between high fidelity of implementation and improved outcomes (although detrimental impact was related to lower fidelity). Published around the same time as Durlak et al.'s (2011) meta-analysis, this study drew considerable attention in the United States and its findings were subjected to immediate scrutiny and criticism (Durlak and Weissberg, 2011).

While there was little direct evidence of theory failure in the SADRC study, it cannot be ruled out, and the authors highlight this as a possible explanation for their findings. In particular, they note the alternative view that 'only a subset of elementary-aged children has deficits in social behavior and character, and these deficits require a more targeted, more intensive intervention than schoolwide programs can provide' (SACDRC, 2010: li). This proposition relates directly to the issue of which children actually directly benefit from universal SEL provision, covered earlier in this chapter. In terms of implementation failure, some analyses suggested that staff in intervention schools failed to use materials and practices in their classrooms significantly more than their counterparts in control schools (Durlak and Weissberg, 2011). However, as noted above, the authors found no association between higher levels of fidelity and improved outcomes in the schools implementing the SEL interventions.

A complicating factor is that the methods through which implementation fidelity was monitored in this study were somewhat problematic (e.g. primarily self-reported implementation data, attempted use of a standardised measure for seven heterogenous programmes). The authors themselves acknowledged that they may have provided insufficient information about whether low fidelity was the cause of the null findings. As a general point, recall that a failure to comprehensively monitor different aspects of implementation can lead to Type III errors (see Chapter 6), and this may be evidenced here. Hence, implementation failure and evaluation failure may have interacted in this particular case.

In addition to the problems in monitoring implementation, the authors noted two other key limitations of their study that provide evidence of possible evaluation failure. Firstly, high levels of missing data (because of lack of parental consent and/ or student assent) meant that around a third of the sample at any one measurement were missing. Lack of background data on students with missing versus complete data meant that the authors were unable to determine whether there were latent differences between these two groups that could have accounted for the overall findings. A second, related issue was the greatly reduced sample sizes for individual evaluations. This meant that the statistical tests employed to determine impact were 'underpowered'. That is, they were less sensitive to differences between the treatment and control groups when individual programmes were examined. However, this does not explain why the authors' main analysis, in which they combined data from the seven trial sites (and hence were more than adequately powered), also produced null results.

Case study 3: Universal and indicated cognitive-behavioural intervention in Australia (Sheffield et al., 2006)

I have included this Australian study as it is the only example I have been able to find where universal, targeted/indicated and integrated universal *and* targeted/indicated provision has been compared to usual practice. The aforementioned PATHS to PAX trial is similar, but only compares integrated provision with usual practice. The authors conducted a cluster randomised controlled trial to examine the impact of cognitive behavioural approaches in preventing depression among *c*.2,500 adolescents attending 34 schools. Around 20 per cent of the sample were identified as 'at risk' following pre-intervention screening. Sheffield et al. (2006) used a range of outcome measures, including assessment of depressive symptoms, social and adaptive functioning and associated difficulties (e.g. anxiety). Data was also collected on programme adherence/fidelity and reach via implementer self-report. The universal intervention was a primarily curriculum-based approach, consisting of eight teacher-led weekly sessions delivered over a school term. The sessions focused on identifying thoughts, feelings and problem situations and the relationship between these, in addition to problem-solving skills. The targeted/indicated intervention comprised a more intensive set of sessions over the same period of time, with a greater focus on interpersonal skills (e.g. assertion, conflict resolution). This level of provision was facilitated by school counsellors and/or external mental health professionals.

The authors reported completely null results across all intervention conditions. That is, the outcomes for students in the universal, targeted/indicated and integrated universal *and* targeted/indicated schools did not differ from those in usual practical control schools. This was the case for both 'at risk' students and their peers. There were also no differences at 12-month follow-up. Implementation data suggested that both programme adherence/fidelity and reach were consistently high.

In terms of theory failure, a key feature of the provision in this study is its brevity. Both the universal and targeted/indicated interventions were relatively brief, comprising only eight weekly sessions. This is discordant with the broader SEL evidence base, in which programmes typically comprise around 40 sessions (Durlak et al., 2011). Furthermore, the average duration of targeted/indicated cognitive-behavioural interventions for depression in adolescents is approximately 18 sessions (Klein et al., 2007). Hence the theory of change for the interventions in the Sheffield et al. (2006) study may have underestimated the exposure/dosage required to produce changes in outcomes in both at-risk students and their peers in the general school population.

There is little direct evidence of implementation failure in this study, as the authors reported that both adherence/fidelity and reach were high in each of the intervention conditions. However, given the potential for implementer self-reports to inflate their estimates of different aspects of implementation (see Chapter 6), a lack of fidelity cannot be ruled out. In terms of reach, attendance ranged from 75 per cent (targeted component) to 90 per cent (universal component). While this may at first seem high, recall that the interventions only lasted for eight sessions. This meant that for the targeted component, participants only attended an average of six sessions, reducing the potential for change even further.

Finally, in terms of evaluation failure, while this study has a number of strengths (such as a large sample, random assignment, etc.), there were a number of limitations that may have influenced its findings. Firstly, the general focus of the outcome measurement battery utilised by the authors was yoked towards detecting treatment effects among at-risk students undergoing targeted intervention (e.g. measurement of depressive symptomology). As Greenberg (2010) has noted, the majority of the school population do not develop/experience difficulties, and as such a 'floor effect' is likely to have occurred in the universal conditions. Furthermore, even though Sheffield et al. (2006) reported data on two aspects of implementation, this was only drawn from around half of the intervention sites and was not modelled against any outcome data.

Using null findings to inform the development of theory, research and practice in SEL

The value of studies that yield null results tends to be misinterpreted in my experience. On the one hand, it can be very easy to dismiss them outright because they appear to counter the SEL orthodoxy. On the other, it can be dangerous to assume that a study yielding null results proves unequivocally that a given SEL programme is ineffective. As we have seen, interpreting these studies requires consideration of theory failure, implementation failure, evaluation failure and the interaction between each of these.

So how can these studies and others like them inform the field? Each of our three case studies were conducted by independent research teams. The fact that each yielded null results might be seen to provide evidence of differential effects in independent studies that have been reported in related fields but have yet to be explored systematically in SEL (see above). It is fair to say that in each study there is evidence to support both the high fidelity and cynical viewpoints proposed by Eisner (2009). So, for example, there were issues raised in relation to implementation in the SACDRC study (high fidelity explanation). However, the authors' analyses indicated that implementation variability did not properly account for variability in outcomes (cynical view).

There are also implications for programme design. The secondary SEAL study provided a field-test of whether an essentially non-prescriptive SEL intervention can yield improved outcomes. Setting aside issues relating to evaluation failure, we might conclude from this study that the programme may be improved with a more prescriptive, directional approach. Similarly, the brevity of the interventions in the Sheffield et al. (2006) study may be seen as providing evidence of a dose-response threshold not having been met, and thus future iterations could be improved via increased frequency/duration of sessions.

These studies also speak to research design issues. Indeed, it is arguably much more common for study designs to be scrutinised when findings are null than when they are positive. In considering the three case studies examined in this chapter, there is much that we can take forward. They all underscore the importance of a comprehensive approach to examining both implementation and outcomes. In terms of the former, monitoring should involve both researcher and implementer reports, ideally more than once, and take into account the full range of implementation factors. In terms of the latter, instrumentation should be informed by programme theory (for example, in selecting a range of theoretically plausible proximal and distal outcomes). Outcome measurement should also be multi-informant in nature to allow for triangulation. Without such an approach to evaluation, it is difficult to rule out competing explanations for study findings. However, studies of such rigour are undoubtedly more costly.

 ## Further Reading

Durlak, J. et al. (2011) 'The impact of enhancing students' social and emotional learning: a meta-analysis of school-based interventions', *Child Development*, 82: 405–32.

Wilson, S. and Lipsey, M. (2007) 'School-based interventions for aggressive and disruptive behaviour: update of a meta-analysis', *American Journal of Preventive Medicine*, 33: S130–43.

8

Conclusion

Overview

In this chapter I draw together and summarise the key themes developed throughout the preceding chapters. I build upon these to make a series of recommendations for future research, including the need for a new wave of effectiveness studies, an increase in high-quality research beyond the United States, a broadening of focus in implementation evaluation and detailed modelling of the cost-benefits and cost-effectiveness of SEL.

Key Points

- Taken as a whole, the evidence base pertaining to SEL is positive, albeit with a variety of limitations, gaps and inconsistencies that limit the strength of any conclusions we may draw.

- SEL is not a fad, nor is it a panacea, and to view or promote it as such may ultimately be detrimental.

- The next generation of research activity in this area needs to address some of the important gaps and inconsistencies that have been highlighted throughout this text, including but not limited to:
    - a new wave of research examining the effectiveness (as opposed to efficacy) of SEL interventions, with a particular focus on the conditions and factors that enable the positive

findings of efficacy trials to be replicated in 'real-world' conditions;

- a substantial increase in high-quality evaluations of SEL activity outside of the United States, whether these relate to cultural adaptations of existing interventions or 'home-grown' programmes;

- a broadening of focus in implementation research to consider factors beyond fidelity/adherence and dosage, such as programme differentiation;

- further empirical investigation of the SEL logic model, such as exploring temporal relationships between proximal and distal variables in an evaluation context;

- more economic analyses of SEL programmes that accurately model their cost-effectiveness and cost-benefits using empirically derived data.

〰️ Points for Reflection

- Taken as a whole, does the evidence base support the emergence of SEL as a dominant orthodoxy in education? Why/why not?

Examining the orthodoxy of SEL

I began this book by stating that SEL is inarguably a, if not *the*, major orthodoxy in contemporary education. As an academic working in the field of educational psychology who has become increasingly engrossed in SEL over the last few years, I was curious to know whether this privileged status was warranted. In England, the rise of SEL came with the introduction of the SEAL programme nationwide during the mid-to-late 2000s. Along with it came an uncritical acceptance not only that SEAL and programmes like it were needed by all schools, but that they would also transform our education system. The benefits of SEL quickly became 'assumed truths', and within a few years SEAL was being implemented in most primary and secondary schools (Humphrey et al., 2010).

One of the primary motivations for writing this book was, therefore, to take a detailed look at SEL and the evidence base on which it rests. I wanted to find out what the research really tells us. However, this would inevitably involve asking some critical questions of an established orthodoxy, and this can be dangerous territory. Gorman (1998), writing about drug prevention policy orthodoxies in the United States, suggests: 'Questions are raised about those who dispute claims of effectiveness . . . the issue becomes not about whether the stated goals and objectives of programs are being met, but the commitment and motives of critics. The burden of proof is placed on them' (p. 119).

However, my aim was not to simply challenge the SEL zeitgeist. I had no interest in 'taking a scalp'. Like other critical voices in the field, I have no doubt that 'engaging with children's social and emotional development is vital, and the contested nature of the concept . . . does not mean that there is not a need for many of the activities taking place on the ground' (Watson et al., 2012: 209).

In writing this book, I sought to examine the various aspects of the field through a critical lens in the hope of being able to provide a balanced, informed assessment. Such an exercise can be a useful means of identifying areas of strength *and* those of weakness. The latter of these, which manifest as gaps in understanding, inconsistencies, methodological issues, etc. can then be addressed as the field moves forward.

So, what are some of the conclusions that have emerged through this process?

1. SEL is very clearly a dominant orthodoxy in education systems across the world, but the current research base does not reflect this. That is, there has been an over-reliance on evidence from the United States. Cultural transferability cannot be assumed.

2. The core concept of SEL and the theory of change underpinning it are fundamentally sound, but there is a distinct lack of clarity in their interpretation and use in the broader discourse. Furthermore, some of the key values and assumptions underpinning SEL may be considered problematic by some.

3. SEL takes different forms in different countries and cultures and there is considerable variation evident in the influence of policy, the role played by research evidence and the level of prescriptiveness inherent in the approaches taken.

4. The assessment of SEL is central to the enhancement of theory, research and practice, but this aspect of the field is relatively underdeveloped. In particular, the crucial distinction between typical and maximal behaviour needs to be explored more fully in relation to SEL.

5. Studying implementation processes and the factors affecting them is a fundamental prerequisite for developing our understanding of SEL interventions more generally. However, this aspect of the field is undermined by a predominantly narrow focus on fidelity/adherence and dosage.

6. Taken as a whole, the evidence base suggests that high-quality universal SEL interventions can be effective in promoting a range of outcomes for children and young people. However, there are numerous issues that suggest that caution in interpretation is required.

Social and emotional learning is not a fad

One of the key questions I raised in the introduction to this text was whether SEL is simply the latest in a series of educational 'fads'. Paul and Elder (2007) suggest that the history of education is littered with examples of the 'comings and goings of quick fixes for deep-seated educational problems'. These fads, they argue, result in the fragmentation of energy and effort in schools, and lead to time and money being wasted.

On the surface, SEL has some of the hallmarks of an educational fad. Firstly, at its core there is a plausible theory, but one that has perhaps been imposed in ways that can be unclear and unhelpful, often because of a 'hijacking' process in which meaning is lost and parameters are stretched ever further. Secondly, it has been embraced enthusiastically by 'ideological advocates'. Thirdly, it has been promoted in some circles as a panacea for all that ails education.

Despite this, my reading of the theory, research, policy and practice in this field leads me to conclude that SEL is not an educational fad. A key issue here is that the 'movement' has exhibited much greater staying power than fad theory would suggest. Even in its contemporary form (e.g. as explicit, universal instruction through formal interventions), SEL has already exceeded the 7–10 year cycle of interest in which education fads come and go (Paul and Elder, 2007). Beyond this, recall that in Chapter 3 we saw evidence of an emphasis on the affective aspect of education (what we might dub 'proto-SEL') going back through the history of schooling. The exact form may have evolved, but the 'essential idea' of SEL has been with us for centuries. This is not a common feature of fads.

A further issue is that despite the gaps and inconsistencies highlighted throughout this text, there is still enough positive evidence to suggest that high-quality, well-implemented SEL can be effective in promoting a range of important outcomes for children and young people. This is not something that one typically sees with fads. Indeed, one of the reasons they fade away is that the accumulating evidence base fails to support their continued popularity.

. . . nor is it a panacea!

However, my reading of the evidence base also leads me to the conclusion that SEL is also not the panacea for all that ails education and/or childhood/youth. Indeed, I see its promotion as a 'cure-all' in the general discourse to be misleading and potentially detrimental (see Chapter 1). Furthermore, the very notion of 'SEL-as-panacea' brings us back to the idea of a youth in crisis. After all, for us to have a 'solution', there must first be a crisis to solve. As we saw in Chapter 3 this is a somewhat problematic view and may in fact serve to promote a deficit model of children's agency (Ecclestone and Hayes, 2008). Finally, the evidence emerging relating to differential outcomes suggests, quite logically, that the impact of any given intervention is unlikely to be uniform and is instead subject to a range of individual and ecological differences pertaining to risk exposure and other factors (Domitrovich et al., 2010b). However, this in itself is not a reason to abandon a universalist approach. As we saw in Chapter 2, even though not all children will necessarily benefit from SEL, a universal approach is more inclusive, less stigmatising and potentially more cost-effective than available alternatives.

Given the above, it is important to qualify statements about the effectiveness of SEL and take a more measured approach in its promotion. Thus, rather than us suggesting that SEL is needed in all schools, we may consider for whom such approaches may be most needed and/or beneficial, why and under what circumstances (Durlak et al., 2011; Weisz et al., 2005). Given this, SEL may be best viewed as a potentially very effective means through which to effect positive change for children and young people, but one that schools may need to consider in terms of their individual contexts. A needs-driven approach may be useful here, in which schools consider questions such as:

- Is there a perceived need for social and emotional learning to be explicitly taught in our school, and if so, why? For example, are members of the student body exposed to high levels of risk?

- What specific outcomes are expected as a result of the adoption of an SEL intervention? How much change is expected? Does the available evidence for the intervention support these expectations?

- What processes and practices are already in place that promote SEL, and to what extent will a given intervention be different from, enhance or complement these? For example, what will be the added value of an adopted programme?

- Is our school ready to implement SEL? How do staff feel about it? Are the necessary human, financial and other resources in place?

- Is the adoption of a given SEL intervention in line with current and future school priorities?

Future directions

The SEL evidence base is large and rapidly expanding, but there is broad agreement that there is still a great deal more work to be done in each of the core areas of SEL addressed in this text. For example, in relation to SEL outcome research, Durlak et al. concluded that 'current findings are not definitive' (2011: 419). Similarly, talking about implementation, Domitrovich et al. noted, 'there are more questions than answers' (2008: 21). Finally, in relation to assessment, Merrell and Gueldner have argued that 'there is a notable lack of good assessment instrumentation available' (2010: 124).

So what should be the specific future priorities for SEL research? For what it is worth, my reading of the literature in preparing and writing this book leads me to believe that the issues outlined below need to be addressed. This is not an exhaustive list. I have included those that I believe are the most crucial to furthering our knowledge about the role and impact of SEL in education.

A focus on rigorous effectiveness trials of established SEL programmes

Much of the SEL research base is comprised of efficacy trials wherein the impact of an intervention is tested under highly controlled, optimal circumstances. This is an important step in establishing if such a programme can change outcomes. However, as noted elsewhere in this book, such trials lack external validity because schools access resources and support not typically available to them (Shucksmith et al., 2009). Add to this the fact that efforts to disseminate and 'scale up' SEL programmes in normal school settings can produce disappointing results (Elias et al., 2003) and it becomes clear that we need much more effectiveness research, or more formally 'Type II translational research' (Greenberg, 2010).

. . . with a focus on factors and conditions that influence success

As part of the new wave of effectiveness research noted above, there should be a focus on empirically modelling the factors and conditions that influence success. We know that schools often fail to replicate the outcomes of efficacy trials in normal contexts. We also have a series of plausible reasons why this may be the case (see factors affecting implementation in Chapter 6), but research on this specific aspect of SEL currently lags behind other areas. Data generation and analysis is therefore needed in order to build a rigorous knowledge base that can be used to inform effective implementation of proven SEL interventions in typical circumstances.

An increase in high-quality SEL research across the world

The United States has led the way in this field, but there is a substantial discord between the origins of the current evidence base and the global reach that SEL now has. As noted earlier, cultural transferability cannot be assumed. A substantial increase is therefore needed in research examining both cultural adaptations of existing programmes and 'home-grown' interventions across the world. Pleasingly, there are signs that this is beginning to happen. In relation to home-grown approaches, the years following the census date (31 December 2007) of Durlak et al.'s SEL meta-analysis have seen evaluations from England (e.g. Humphrey et al., 2010; Wigelsworth et al., 2012), Australia (e.g. Dix et al., 2012), Sweden (e.g. Kimber et al., 2008) and elsewhere. Similarly, evaluations of cultural adaptations of existing programmes have also started to emerge more frequently. For example, Malti et al. (2011) field-tested a cultural adaptation of the PATHS programme in Switzerland. Obviously, such trends should continue, and the accumulated evidence base this produces should serve to deepen and enhance our knowledge about SEL.

A broadening of focus in research on implementation processes and practices

As we saw in Chapter 6, the process of implementation is the fulcrum on which the success of an SEL programme rests. As Durlak et al. state, 'developing an evidence-based intervention is an essential but insufficient condition for success; the program must also be well executed' (2011: 418). In examining the literature on implementation, I was struck by how little empirical evidence there was available on several key aspects. For example, there has been remarkably little attention paid to programme differentiation. Yet, knowing about the existing social-emotional processes and practices in schools that provide the foundation upon which an intervention sits is surely a fundamental consideration. After all, schools do not implement new SEL interventions in a vacuum. We know that most (if not all) are already likely to be implementing SEL in some way or another. Recall that around 90 per cent of school leaders reported engaging in a variety of classroom and school-wide activities designed to promote SEL in the SACDRC (2010) study in the United States. Similarly, in a recent scoping survey in England schools reported using up to 13 different approaches as part of their attempts to promote emotional well-being (Vostanis et al., 2012). How does variation in such practices influence the successful integration of a universal SEL programme?

There are numerous questions relating to different aspects of implementation that need to be answered through future research activities. In relation to the fidelity-adaptation debate, we need to know much more about the critical versus desirable aspects of different programmes, and indeed the nature of adaptations made by implementers and their influence on programme outcomes. Similarly, variation in implementer behaviour (e.g. quality) and participant responsiveness remain underexplored. Perhaps most importantly, research which incorporates implementation needs to take a comprehensive approach in order to avoid Type III errors (see Chapter 6).

I would also argue that future research should focus much more on the issue of teachers' 'will and skill' as primary drivers of SEL implementation. Common sense suggests that how teachers feel about SEL and their own social and emotional skills will play an important role in their implementation efforts and subsequent student outcomes, and authors such as Jennings and Greenberg (2009) have provided plausible models for the mechanisms that may underpin these processes. However, there have only been a limited number of studies that have begun to explore these and other, related hypotheses.

Examination of integrated models of provision

The primary focus of this text has been on universal SEL as opposed to targeted and/or indicated interventions. Yet we know that schools can and do work at each of these different levels in their efforts to promote positive outcomes for students. Indeed, some of the more recently developed programmes (e.g. SEAL in England, KidsMatter in Australia) incorporate an 'integrated' model of provision. Domitrovich et al. (2010b) provide a compelling account of the logic and theory underpinning such frameworks, yet there remains a poverty of evidence that examines their effectiveness in a rigorous and systematic manner. To date, only a couple of studies have ventured into this territory – examples being the ongoing PATHS to PAX study (Domitrovich et al., 2010b) and the Sheffield et al. (2006) evaluation that was one of our case studies in Chapter 7. A key priority for future research in SEL is therefore work that is able to unpick the influence of different components of an integrated model (e.g. usual practice versus universal provision, targeted/indicated provision and integrated/combined provision).

Explicit testing of the SEL logic model as part of programme evaluation

As we saw in Chapter 2, despite some inconsistencies there is a growing body of empirical evidence that supports the key propositions outlined in the SEL logic model (CASEL, 2007). However, this evidence base has been constructed in a somewhat piecemeal fashion. Despite the fact that it is commonplace for SEL evaluations to examine a range of factors and outcomes directly applicable to the logic model, few (if any) examine whether these relate to one another in ways that are consistent with it. Indeed, Durlak et al. noted, 'more rigorous research on the presumed mediational role of SEL skill development is also warranted. Only a few studies tested and found a temporal relation between skill enhancement and other positive outcomes' (2011: 419). Research which empirically tests the SEL logic model as part of programme evaluation will therefore make a significant contribution to our understanding of *how* proximal (e.g. social and emotional skills) and distal (e.g. academic performance) variables relate to one another and the factors that mediate them (e.g. attachment to school).

More research on the impact of SEL on academic outcomes

The evidence pointing to a potential impact on academic progress as a distal outcome of SEL is promising but there remain many unanswered questions. Furthermore, the number of studies that have included an academic outcome is only a very small proportion of the overall field (e.g. less than one in five). As noted in Chapter 7, the conclusions that can be drawn regarding the 'pure' influence of SEL on academics is arguably confounded by the explicit academic content of a number of programmes. Thus it is difficult to conclude whether children's progress is the result of processes hypothesised in the SEL logic model or simply because they received additional academic instruction as part of the intervention in which they participated. Ultimately, this issue may become more important over time, as an increasing number of programmes seek to integrate explicit academic components as part of the package of provision on offer (see, for example, the 4Rs programme reported by Jones et al., 2010). Hence further research is needed to begin to explore how the impact of SEL varies as a function of differing levels of academic content infused into programmes.

Further development of the assessment science of SEL

Accurate assessment is pivotal to the theory, research and practice of SEL. It pervades every single aspect of the field, and yet in some ways it is an area where considerable development is needed. For example, there is no shortage of available measures, but there is considerable variability in their implementation characteristics and psychometric properties (Humphrey et al., 2011). This may be a contributory factor in the finding that only around a third of SEL evaluations actually report social and emotional skills as an outcome (Durlak et al., 2011). A range of related issues also require further exploration. We need to know more about the relationship between typical and maximal behaviour in relation to SEL. Research on trait and ability emotional intelligence, the underlying constructs of these two contrasting approaches to assessment, suggests that they are two distinct entities that may be subject to different influences and relate to distal outcomes (such as mental health) in different ways. Where they are assessed together in SEL evaluations they can produce contrasting findings (see, for example, Humphrey et al., 2008), which raises the question as to which of the two protocols should be given priority in determining whether a given intervention has been 'successful'. On a similar note, we know that different informants (e.g. children, teachers, parents) can produce variable ratings of social and emotional competence.

This is to be expected since they each bring something unique to the table in terms of their frames of reference, but this issue needs to be explored more fully because it has implications for determining whether an intervention can be judged to have succeeded. At the very least, these issues reinforce the need for future studies to use multi-informant, multi-source data in the assessment and monitoring of SEL.

Economics

The economics of SEL is perhaps the area of which we know least. One widely publicised report on the estimated costs and benefits of early intervention, which included several SEL interventions, suggested that the benefits outweighed the costs per participant (see Chapter 7). However, there has been a dearth of published studies in the academic literature that explicitly model the cost-benefits and/or cost-effectiveness of SEL (Hummel et al., 2009; McCabe, 2008). Thus future research should consider the required inputs of SEL relative to outputs expressed in monetary terms (cost-benefit analysis) and key domains such as health-related quality of life (cost-effectiveness analysis). Such research will make a significant contribution to the field and have great practical utility in terms of helping schools to make informed decisions about whether a given programme represents a sound investment.

Testing of a differential gains hypothesis

Where research has considered the role of individual differences/ characteristics in determining responsiveness to SEL interventions (e.g. Ashdown and Bernard, 2011; Conduct Problems Prevention Research Group, 1999; Slee et al., 2009) there is evidence to support a differential (as opposed to universal) gains hypothesis. This is, of course, directly in line with the risk and resilience framework that has been a key influence on the development of SEL (see Chapter 3). Future research should therefore consider sub-group analyses of factors such as sex, ethnicity, socio-economic status and special educational needs as a matter of course (Durlak et al., 2011). There is also a pressing need to take further into account the role of school and familial differences. For example, one can see the potential for interesting school–individual interactions (e.g. it may be that SEL provides a protective resource for high-risk students in certain school contexts but not others). Such work will undoubtedly advance the developing SEL knowledge base and provide greater understanding of the specific process underpinning positive change for children and young people.

 Points for Reflection

- Which of the above future directions should be prioritised? Why?

Final thoughts

SEL is a global phenomenon that has captured the imagination of academics, policy-makers and practitioners alike in recent years. It is perhaps fair to say that its growth in popularity has been faster than the development of the evidence base upon which it rests. However, this is changing. While interest in SEL 'at the chalkface' has arguably stabilised, research in the field is still rapidly expanding. For example, I was told recently that somewhere in the region of 50 SEL studies have been published since the census date of Durlak et al.'s (2011) seminal meta-analysis. This creates some difficulties in attempting to write a book that presents an up-to-date overview of the field as each new week seems to bring new evidence that is relevant to one or more substantive areas! This issue aside, the fact that research is flourishing means that future years are likely to bring ever greater advancements in our knowledge and understanding of SEL, which will inevitably lead to refinements in how it is practised in schools. Ultimately, this promises a brighter future for children and young people.

 Further Reading

Greenberg, M. (2010) 'School-based prevention: current status and future challenges', *Effective Education*, 2: 27–52.

References

Adi, Y., Kiloran, A., Janmohamed, K. and Stewart-Brown, S. (2007) *Systematic Review of the Effectiveness of Interventions to Promote Mental Wellbeing in Children in Primary Education.* Warwick: University of Warwick.

Ainley, J., Withers, G., Underwood, C. and Frigo, T. (2006) *National Survey of Health and Wellbeing Promotion Policies and Practices in Secondary Schools.* Melbourne: Australian Council for Educational Research.

Ainscow, M., Booth, T. and Dyson, A. (2006) 'Inclusion and the standards agenda: negotiating policy pressures in England', *International Journal of Inclusive Education,* 10 (4–5): 295–308.

Aos, S., Lieb, R., Mayfield, J., Miller, M. and Pennucci, A. (2004) *Benefits and Costs of Prevention and Early Intervention Programs for Youth.* Olympia, WA: Washington State Institute for Public Policy.

Ashdown, D. M. and Bernard, M. E. (2011) 'Can explicit instruction in social and emotional learning skills benefit the social-emotional development, well-being, and academic achievement of young children?', *Early Childhood Education Journal,* 39 (6): 397–405.

August, G. J., Bloomquist, M. L., Lee, S. S., Realmuto, G. M. and Hektner, J. M. (2006) 'Can evidence-based prevention programs be sustained in community practice settings? The Early Risers' Advanced-Stage Effectiveness Trial', *Prevention Science,* 7 (2): 151–65.

Austin, E. J., Farrelly, D., Black, C. and Moore, H. (2007) 'Emotional intelligence, Machiavellianism and emotional manipulation: Does EI have a dark side?', *Personality and Individual Differences,* 43 (1): 179–89.

Australian Council for Educational Research (2010) *MindMatters Evaluation Report.* Camberwell, Vic.: ACER.

Australian Government Department of Health and Ageing (2009) *Overview of the KidsMatter Primary Initiative: Framework, Components and Implementation Details. World Health.* Canberra: AGDHA.

Bar-On, R. and Parker, J. (2008) *Bar-On Emotional Quotient Inventory: Youth Version (EQi-YV): Technical Manual.* Toronto: Multi-Health Systems.

Battistich, V., Solomon, D., Kim, D.-I., Watson, M. and Schaps, E. (1995) 'Schools as communities, poverty levels of student populations, and students' attitudes, motives, and performance: a multilevel analysis', *American Educational Research Journal*, 32 (3): 627–58.

Battistich, V., Watson, M., Solomon, D., Lewis, C. and Schaps, E. (1999) 'Beyond the three R's: a broader agenda for school reform', *Elementary School Journal*, 99 (5): 415.

Battistich, V., Schaps, E., Watson, M., Solomon, D. and Lewis, C. (2000) 'Effects of the Child Development Project on students' drug use and other problem behaviors', *Journal of Primary Prevention*, 21 (1): 75–99.

Baumeister, R. (2005) *Rethinking Self-Esteem*. Stanford, CA: Stanford Social Innovation Review.

BBC (2011) 'Analysis – testing the emotions'. Retrieved from http://www.bbc.co.uk/programmes/b00z5bqd.

Biggert, J., Kildee, D. and Ryan, T. (2011) *H. R. 2347 Academic, Social and Emotional Learning Act of 2011*. Washington, DC: United States Congress.

Blank, L., Baxter, S., Goyder, L., Guillaume, L., Wilkinson, A., Hummel, S. and Chilcott, J. (2009) *Systematic Review of the Effectiveness of Universal Interventions Which Aim to Promote Emotional and Social Wellbeing in Secondary Schools*. Sheffield: University of Sheffield.

Blank, L., Baxter, S., Goyder, L., Guillaume, L., Wilkinson, A., Hummel, S. and Chilcott, J. (2010) 'Promoting wellbeing by changing behaviour: a systematic review and narrative synthesis of the effectiveness of whole secondary school behavioural interventions', *Mental Health Review Journal*, 15 (2): 43–53.

Brackett, M. (2006) 'Emotional intelligence in the classroom: skill-based training for teachers and students', in J. Ciarrochi and J. D. Mayer (eds), *Applying Emotional Intelligence: A Practitioner's Guide*. New York: Psychology Press, pp. 1–27.

Brackett, M. A., Reyes, M. R., Rivers, S. E., Elbertson, N. A. and Salovey, P. (2012) 'Assessing teachers' beliefs about social and emotional learning', *Journal of Psychoeducational Assessment*, 30 (3): 219–36.

Bradshaw, J. (2011) *The Wellbeing of Children in the UK*, 3rd edn. Bristol: Policy Press.

Branden, N. (1969) *The Psychology of Self-Esteem*. New York: Bantam.

Bryant, A. and Schulenberg, J. (2003) 'How academic achievement, attitudes, and behaviors relate to the course of substance use during adolescence: a 6-year, multiwave national longitudinal study', *Journal of Research on Adolescence*, 13 (3): 361–97.

California Self-Esteem Taskforce (1990) *Toward a State of Self-Esteem: The Final Report of the California Task Force to Promote Self-Esteem and Personal and Social Responsibility*. Sacramento, CA: CTF.

Campbell, M. (2000) 'Framework for design and evaluation of complex interventions to improve health', *British Medical Journal*, 321 (7262): 694–6.

Caplan, G. (1964) *Principles of Preventive Psychiatry*. Oxford: Basic Books.

Carroll, C., Patterson, M., Wood, S., Booth, A., Rick, J. and Balain, S. (2007) 'A conceptual framework for implementation fidelity', *Implementation Science*, 2: 40–9.

CASEL (2003) *Safe and Sound: An Educational Leader's Guide to Evidence-Based Social and Emotional Learning Programs*. Chicago: CASEL.

CASEL (2004) *CASEL: The First Ten Years 1994–2004*. Chicago: CASEL.

CASEL (2007) *How Evidence-Based SEL Programs Work to Produce Greater Student Success in School and Life*. Chicago: CASEL.

Castro, F. G., Barrera, M. and Martinez, C. R. (2004) 'The cultural adaptation of prevention interventions: resolving tensions between fidelity and fit', *Prevention Science*, 5 (1): 41–5.

Centers for Disease Control and Prevention (1999) 'Framework for program evaluation in public health', *Morbidity and Mortality Weekly Report*, 48: 1–45.

Centers for Disease Control and Prevention (2010) 'Youth risk behaviour surveillance – United States, 2009', *Morbidity and Mortality Weekly Report*, 59: 1–36.

Century, J., Rudnick, M. and Freeman, C. (2010) 'A framework for measuring fidelity of implementation: a foundation for shared language and accumulation of knowledge', *American Journal of Evaluation*, 31 (2): 199–218.

Challen, A., Noden, P., West, A. and Machin, S. (2011) *UK Resilience Programme: Final Report*. Nottingham: Department for Education.

Children's Society (2012) *The Good Childhood Report 2012*. Leeds: Children's Society.

Clark, A. F., O'Malley, A., Woodham, A., Barrett, B. and Byford, S. (2005) 'Children with complex mental health problems: needs, costs and predictors over one year', *Child and Adolescent Mental Health*, 10 (4): 170–8.

Clarke, A., Putz, R., Friede, T., Ashdown, J., Adi, Y., Martin, S., Flynn, P. et al. (2010) *Warwick-Edinburgh Mental Well-being Scale (WEMWBS) Acceptability and Validation in English and Scottish Secondary School Students (The WAVES Project)*. Edinburgh: University of Edinburgh.

Cohen, J. (1992) 'A power primer', *Psychological Bulletin*, 112 (1): 155–9.

Cohen, J. (1993) 'The earth is round (p < .05)', *American Psychologist*, 49 (12): 997–1003.

Cohen, J. (2006) 'Social, emotional, ethical, and academic education: creating a climate for learning, participation in democracy, and well-being', *Harvard Educational Review*, 76 (2): 201–37.

Coie, J. D., Dodge, K. A. and Coppotelli, H. (1982) 'Dimensions and types of social status: a cross-age perspective', *Developmental Psychology*, 18 (4): 557–70.

Committee for Children (2011) *Review of Research: Second Step Program (Kindergarten-Grade 5)*. Seattle, WA: CFC.

Commonwealth of Australia (2009) *Overview of the KidsMatter Primary Initiative*. Canberra: CWA.

Conduct Problems Prevention Research Group (1999) 'Initial impact of the Fast Track prevention trial for conduct problems: I. The high-risk sample', *Journal of Consulting and Clinical Psychology*, 67 (5): 631–47.

Connolly, P., Sibbett, C., Hanratty, J., Kerr, K., O'Hare, L. and Winter, K. (2011) *Pupils' Emotional Health and Wellbeing: A Review of Audit Tools and a Survey of Practice in Northern Ireland Post-Primary Schools*. Belfast: Queen's University.

Connor, B., Small, S. A. and Cooney, S. M. (2007) *Program Fidelity and Adaptation: Meeting Local Needs Without Compromising Program Effectiveness*. Madison, WI: University of Wisconsin.

Cook, T. D., Habib, F., Phillips, M., Settersten, R. A., Shagle, S. C., Degirmencioglu, S. M. and Richard, A. (1999) 'Comer's School Development Program in Prince George's County, Maryland: theory-based evaluation', *American Educational Research Journal*, 36 (3): 543–97.

Cooke, M. B., Ford, J., Levine, J., Bourke, C., Newell, L. and Lapidus, G. (2007) 'The effects of city-wide implementation of "Second Step" on elementary school students' prosocial and aggressive behaviors', *Journal of Primary Prevention*, 28 (2): 93–115.

Craig, C. (2007) *The Potential Dangers of a Systematic, Explicit Approach to Teaching Social and Emotional Skills (SEAL)*. Glasgow: Centre for Confidence and Wellbeing.

Crepeau, I. M. and Richards, M. A. (2003) *A Show of Hands: Using Puppets with Young Children*. St Paul, MN: Redleaf Press.

CSVP (2006) *Model Programs Fact Sheet: Promoting Alternative Thinking Strategies*. Boulder, CO: University of Colorado.

Curtis, C. and Norgate, R. (2007) 'An evaluation of the PATHS curriculum at Key Stage 1', *Educational Psychology in Practice*, 23: 33–44.

Dahlin, B. (2008) 'Social and emotional education in Sweden: two examples of good practice', in C. Clouder (ed.), *Social and Emotional Education: An International Analysis*. Santander, Spain: Marcelino Botín Foundation, pp. 85–116.

Daly, B. P., Burke, R., Hare, I., Mills, C., Owens, C., Moore, E. and Weist, M. D. (2006) 'Enhancing No Child Left Behind school mental health connections', *Journal of School Health*, 76 (9): 446–51.

Davis, S. and Humphrey, N. (2012a) 'Emotional intelligence predicts adolescent mental health beyond personality and cognitive ability', *Personality and Individual Differences*, 52 (2): 144–9.

Davis, S. K. and Humphrey, N. (2012b) 'Emotional intelligence as a moderator of stressor–mental health relations in adolescence: evidence for specificity', *Personality and Individual Differences*, 52 (2): 100–5.

Denham, S. A. (2005) *Assessing Social-Emotional Development in Children from a Longitudinal Perspective for the National Children's Study*. Columbus, OH: Batelle Memorial Institute.

Denham, S. A. and Brown, C. (2010) '"Plays nice with others": social-emotional learning and academic success', *Early Education and Development*, 21 (5): 652–80.

Denham, S. A. and Weissberg, R. P. (2004) 'Social-emotional learning in early childhood: what we know and where to go from here', in E. Chesebrough, P. King, T. P. Gullotta and M. Bloom (eds), *A Blueprint for the Promotion of Prosocial Behaviour in Early Childhood*. New York: Kluwer, pp. 13–50.

Denham, S. A., Ji, P. and Hamre, B. (2010) *Compendium of Preschool Through Elementary School Social-Emotional Learning and Associated Assessment Measures*. Chicago: CASEL/University of Illinois.

Denham, S., Wyatt, T. M., Bassett, H. H., Echeverria, D. and Knox, S. S. (2009) 'Assessing social-emotional development in children from a longitudinal perspective', *Journal of Epidemiology and Community Health*, 63 (Suppl. I): i37–52.

Department for Children, Schools and Families (2007) *Social and Emotional Aspects of Learning (SEAL) Programme: Guidance for Secondary Schools*. Nottingham: DCSF Publications.

Department for Education and Skills (2003) *Every Child Matters*. Nottingham: DfES Publications.

Department for Education and Skills (2005a) *Primary Social and Emotional Aspects of Learning (SEAL): Guidance for Schools*. Nottingham: DfES Publications.

Department for Education and Skills (2005b) *Excellence and Enjoyment: Social and Emotional Aspects of Learning*. Nottingham: DfES Publications.

Department for Education and Skills (2006) *Excellence and Enjoyment: Social and Emotional Aspects of Learning (Key Stage 2 Small Group Activities)*. Nottingham: DfES Publications.

Department for Education and Skills (2007a) *Social and Emotional Aspects of Learning for Secondary Schools (SEAL) Guidance Booklet*. Nottingham: DfES Publications.

Department for Education and Skills (2007b) *Social and Emotional Aspects of Learning (SEAL) for Secondary Schools: Tools for Monitoring, Profiling and Evaluation*. Nottingham: DfES Publications.

Department for Education in Northern Ireland (2007) *Progression in Personal Development and Mutual Understanding*. Belfast: DENI.

Dewey, J. (1897) 'My pedagogic creed', *School Journal*, 54 (1): 77–80.

Diamond, A. (2010) 'The evidence base for improving school outcomes by addressing the whole child and by addressing skills and attitudes, not just content', *Early Education and Development*, 21 (5): 780–93.

Dix, K. L., Keeves, J. P., Slee, P., Lawson, M. J., Russell, A., Askell-Williams, H., Skrzypiec, G. et al. (2010) *KidsMatter Primary Evaluation: Technical Report and User Guide*. Adelaide: Shannon Research Press.

Dix, K. L., Slee, P. T., Lawson, M. J. and Keeves, J. P. (2012) 'Implementation quality of whole-school mental health promotion and students' academic performance', *Child and Adolescent Mental Health*, 17 (1): 45–51.

Dixon, T. (2012) 'Educating the emotions from Gradgrind to Goleman', *Research Papers in Education*, 27 (4): 481–95.

Dodge, K. A., McClaskey, C. L. and Feldman, E. (1985) 'Situational approach to the assessment of social competence in children', *Journal of Consulting and Clinical Psychology*, 53 (3): 344–53.

Domitrovich, C. and Greenberg, M. T. (2000) 'The study of implementation: current findings from effective programs that prevent mental disorders in school-aged children', *Journal of Educational and Psychological Consultation*, 11 (2): 193–221.

Domitrovich, C. E., Cortes, R. C. and Greenberg, M. T. (2007) 'Improving young children's social and emotional competence: a randomized trial of the preschool "PATHS" curriculum', *Journal of Primary Prevention*, 28 (2): 67–91.

Domitrovich, C. E., Bradshaw, C. P., Poduska, J. M., Hoagwood, K., Buckley, J. A., Olin, S., Hunter, L. et al. (2008) 'Maximising the implementation quality of evidence-based preventive interventions in schools: a conceptual framework', *Advances in School Mental Health Promotion*, 1 (3): 6–28.

Domitrovich, C. E., Gest, S. D., Gill, S., Jones, D. and DeRousie, R. S. (2009) 'Individual factors associated with professional development training outcomes of the Head Start REDI Program', *Early Education and Development*, 20 (3): 402–30.

Domitrovich, C. E., Gest, S. D., Jones, D., Gill, S. and DeRousie, R. M.

S. (2010a) 'Implementation quality: lessons learned in the context of the Head Start REDI trial', *Early Childhood Research Quarterly*, 25 (3): 284–98.

Domitrovich, C. E., Bradshaw, C. P., Greenberg, M. T., Embry, D., Poduska, J. M. and Ialongo, N. S. (2010b) 'Integrated models of school-based prevention: logic and theory', *Psychology in the Schools*, 47 (1): 71–88.

Dufrene, B., Noell, G. and Gilbertson, D. (2005) 'Monitoring implementation of reciprocal peer tutoring: identifying and intervening with students who do not maintain accurate implementation', *School Psychology*, 34 (1): 74–86.

Duncan, G. J. and Magnuson, K. (2007) 'Penny wise and effect size foolish', *Child Development Perspectives*, 1 (1): 46–51.

Duncan, G. J., Dowsett, C. J., Claessens, A., Magnuson, K., Huston, A. C., Klebanov, P., Pagani, L. S. et al. (2007) 'School readiness and later achievement', *Developmental Psychology*, 43 (6): 1428–46.

Durlak, J. A. (1991) 'Methodology: a practitioner's guide to meta-analysis', *American Journal of Community Psychology*, 19 (3): 291–332.

Durlak, J. A. (1995) *School-Based Prevention Programs for Children and Adolescents*. Thousand Oaks, CA: Sage.

Durlak, J. A. (1997) *Successful Prevention Programs for Children and Adolescents*. New York: Plenum.

Durlak, J. A. (2010) 'The importance of doing well in whatever you do: a commentary on the special edition, "Implementation Research in Early Childhood Education"', *Early Childhood Research Quarterly*, 25 (3): 348–57.

Durlak, J. A. and DuPre, E. P. (2008) 'Implementation matters: a review of research on the influence of implementation on program outcomes and the factors affecting implementation', *American Journal of Community Psychology*, 41 (3–4): 327–50.

Durlak, J. A. and Weissberg, R. P. (2011) 'Promoting social and emotional development is an essential part of students' education', *Human Development*, 54 (1): 1–3.

Durlak, J. A., Weissberg, R. P. and Pachan, M. (2010) 'A meta-analysis of after-school programs that seek to promote personal and social skills in children and adolescents', *American Journal of Community Psychology*, 45 (3–4): 294–309.

Durlak, J. A., Weissberg, R. P., Dymnicki, A. B., Taylor, R. D. and Schellinger, K. B. (2011) 'The impact of enhancing students' social and emotional learning: a meta-analysis of school-based universal interventions', *Child Development*, 82 (1): 405–32.

Dusenbury, L., Brannigan, R., Falco, M. and Hansen, W. B. (2003) 'A review of research on fidelity of implementation: implications for drug abuse prevention in school settings', *Health Education Research*, 18 (2): 237–56.

Dusenbury, L., Zadrazil, J., Mart, A. and Weissberg, R. (2011) *State Learning Standards to Advance Social and Emotional Learning*. Chicago: CASEL.

Ecclestone, K. (2007) 'Resisting images of the "diminished self": the implications of emotional well-being and emotional engagement in education policy', *Journal of Education Policy*, 22 (4): 455–70.

Ecclestone, K. and Hayes, D. (2008) *The Dangerous Rise of Therapeutic Education*. London: Routledge.

Ecclestone, K. and Hayes, D. (2009) 'Changing the subject: the educational implications of developing emotional wellbeing', *Oxford Review of Education*, 35 (3): 371–89.

Eisner, M. (2009) 'No effects in independent prevention trials: can we reject the cynical view?', *Journal of Experimental Criminology*, 5 (2): 163–83.

Elbertson, N. A., Brackett, M. A. and Weissberg, R. P. (2010) 'School-based social and emotional learning (SEL) programming: current perspectives', in A. Hargreaves, A. Lieberman, M. Fullan and D. Hopkins (eds), *Second International Handbook of Educational Change*. New York: Springer, pp. 1017–32.

Elias, M. (1997) 'The missing piece: making the case for greater attention to social and emotional learning', *Education Week*, 17 (5): 36–8.

Elias, M. (2009) 'Social-emotional and character development and academics as a dual focus of educational policy', *Educational Policy*, 23 (6): 831–46.

Elias, M. J., Zins, J. E., Graczyk, P. and Weissberg, R. P. (2003) 'Implementation, sustainability, and scaling up of social-emotional and academic innovations in public schools', *School Psychology Review*, 32 (3): 303–19.

Elias, M. J., Gara, M., Ubriaco, M., Rothbaum, P. A., Clabby, J. F. and Schuyler, T. (1986) 'Impact of a preventive social problem solving intervention on children's coping with middle-school stressors', *American Journal of Community Psychology*, 14 (3): 259–75.

Eliot, M., Cornell, D., Gregory, A. and Fan, X. (2010) 'Supportive school climate and student willingness to seek help for bullying and threats of violence', *Journal of School Psychology*, 48 (6): 533–53.

Eraut, G. and Whiting, R. (2008) *What Do We Mean by Wellbeing? And Why Might It Matter?* Nottingham: DSCF Publications.

Esbensen, F.-A., Miller, M. H., Taylor, T., He, N. and Freng, A. (1999) 'Differential attrition rates and active parental consent', *Evaluation Review*, 23 (3): 316–35.

Evans, C., Margison, F. and Barkham, M. (1998) 'The contribution of reliable and clinically significant change methods to evidence-based mental health', *Evidence-Based Mental Health*, 1 (3): 70–3.

Flay, B. R., Biglan, A., Boruch, R. F., Castro, F. G., Gottfredson, D., Kellam, S., Mościcki, E. K. et al. (2005) 'Standards of evidence: criteria for efficacy, effectiveness and dissemination', *Prevention Science*, 6 (3): 151–75.

Forman, S., Olin, S., Hoagwood, K. and Crowe, M. (2009) 'Evidence-based interventions in schools: developers' views of implementation barriers and facilitators', *School Mental Health*, 1 (1): 26–36.

Frederickson, N. and Cline, T. (2009) *Special Educational Needs, Inclusion and Diversity: A Textbook*, 2nd edn. Buckingham: Open University Press.

Frederickson, N. and Graham, B. (1999) *Social Skills and Emotional Intelligence*. Windsor: NfER Nelson.

Frey, K. S., Hirschstein, M. K., Snell, J. L., Edstrom, L. V. S., MacKenzie, E. P. and Broderick, C. J. (2005) 'Reducing playground bullying and supporting beliefs: an experimental trial of the Steps to Respect program', *Developmental Psychology*, 41 (3): 479–90.

Furedi, F. (2003) *Therapy Culture: Cultivating Vulnerability in an Uncertain Age*. London: Routledge.

Furedi, F. (2009) *Wasted: Why Education Isn't Educating*. London: Continuum.

Gardner, H. (1983) *Frames of Mind: The Theory of Multiple Intelligences*. New York: Basic Books.

Goldberg Lillehoj, C. J., Griffin, K. W. and Spoth, R. (2004) 'Program provider and observer ratings of school-based preventive intervention implementation: agreement and relation to youth outcomes', *Health Education and Behavior*, 31 (2): 242–57.

Goldsmith, H. H., Pollak, S. D. and Davidson, R. J. (2008) 'Developmental neuroscience perspectives on emotion regulation', *Child Development Perspectives*, 2 (3): 132–40.

Goleman, D. (1996) *Emotional Intelligence: Why It Can Matter More Than IQ*. London: Bloomsbury.

Goodman, R. (1997) 'The Strengths and Difficulties Questionnaire: a research note', *Journal of Child Psychology and Psychiatry*, 38 (5): 581–6.

Gorman, D. M. (1998) 'The irrelevance of evidence in the development of school-based drug prevention policy, 1986–1996', *Evaluation Review*, 22 (1): 118–46.

Gottfredson, D. C. and Gottfredson, G. D. (2002) 'Quality of school-based prevention programs: results from a national survey', *Journal of Research in Crime and Delinquency*, 39 (1): 3–35.

Graczyk, P. A., Weissberg, R. P., Payton, J. W., Elias, M. J., Greenberg, M. T. and Zins, J. E. (2000) 'Criteria for evaluating the quality of school-based social and emotional learning programs', in R. Bar-On and J. Parker (eds), *The Handbook of Emotional Intelligence: Theory, Development, Assessment, and Application at Home, School, and in the Workplace*. San Francisco: Wiley, pp. 391–410.

Green, H., McGinnity, A., Meltzer, H., Ford, T. and Goodman, R. (2005) *Mental Health of Children and Young People in Great Britain*. Cardiff: Office for National Statistics.

Greenberg, M. T. (2010) 'School-based prevention: current status and future challenges', *Effective Education*, 2 (1): 27–52.

Greenberg, M. T. and Kusche, C. A. (1993) *Promoting Social and Emotional Development in Deaf Children: The PATHS Project*. Seattle, WA: University of Washington Press.

Greenberg, M. T., Kusche, C. A., Cook, E. T. and Quamma, J. P. (1995) 'Promoting emotional competence in school-aged children: the effects of the PATHS curriculum', *Development and Psychopathology*, 7 (1): 117–36.

Greenberg, M. T., Kusche, C. A. and Riggs, N. R. (2004) 'The PATHS curriculum: theory and research on neurocognitive development and school success', in J. E. Zins (ed.), *Building Academic Success on Social and Emotional Learning: What Does the Research Say?* New York: Teachers College Press, pp. 170–88.

Greenberg, M. T., Domitrovich, C. E., Graczyk, P. A. and Zins, J. E. (2005) *The Study of Implementation in School-Based Preventive Interventions: Theory, Research, and Practice*. Rockville, MD: CMHS.

Gresham, F. M. and Elliot, S. N. (2008) *Social Skills Improvement System: Rating Scales Manual*. Minneapolis, MN: Pearson.

Gross, J. (2010) 'SEAL and the changing national education agenda', *Keynote Presented at the 4th Annual Secondary SEAL Conference*. London: Optimus Education.

Gross, J. J. and Muñoz, R. F. (1995) 'Emotion regulation and mental health', *Clinical Psychology: Science and Practice*, 2 (2): 151–64.

Guldberg, H. (2009) *Reclaiming Childhood: Freedom and Play in an Age of Fear*. London: Routledge.

Haddon, A., Goodman, H., Park, J. and Crick, R. D. (2005) 'Evaluating emotional literacy in schools: the development of the School Emotional Environment for Learning Survey', *Pastoral Care in Education*, 23 (4): 5–16.

Hage, S. M. and Romano, J. L. (2010) 'History of prevention and prevention groups: legacy for the 21st century', *Group Dynamics: Theory, Research, and Practice*, 14 (3): 199–210.

Hallam, S., Rhamie, J. and Shaw, J. (2006) *Evaluation of the Primary Behaviour and Attendance Pilot*. Nottingham: DfES Publications.

Harvey, J. and Delfabbro, P. H. (2004) 'Psychological resilience in disadvantaged youth: a critical overview', *Australian Psychologist*, 39 (1): 3–13.

Hattie, J. (2009) *Visible Learning*. London: Routledge.

Hattie, J. (2012) *Visible Learning for Teachers: Maximising Impact on Learning*. London: Routledge.

Havighurst, R. J. (1974) 'Youth in crisis', *School Review*, 83 (1): 5–10.

Hawkins, J. D., Catalano, R. F., Morrison, D. M., O'Donnell, J., Abbott, R. D. and Day, L. E. (1992) 'The Seattle Social Development Project: effects of the first four years on protective factors and problem behaviors', in J. McCord and R. E. Tremblay (eds), *Preventing Antisocial Behavior: Interventions from Birth Through Adolescence*. New York: Guilford Press, pp. 139–61.

Hayes, W. (2006) *The Progressive Education Movement: Is It Still a Factor in Today's Schools?* Lanham, MD: R&L Education.

Henry, J. (2011) 'Lessons in Cheryl Cole replace history and geography lessons', *The Telegraph*, 3 September.

Herrnstein, R. J. and Murray, C. (1994) *The Bell Curve: Intelligence and Class Structure in American Life*. New York: Free Press.

Hill, C., Bloom, H., Black, A. R. and Lipsey, M. W. (2008) 'Empirical benchmarks for interpreting effect sizes in research', *Child Development Perspectives*, 2 (3): 172–7.

Hoffman, D. M. (2009) 'Reflecting on social emotional learning: a critical perspective on trends in the United States', *Review of Educational Research*, 79 (2): 533–56.

Holsen, I., Iversen, A. C. and Smith, B. H. (2009) 'Universal social competence promotion programme in school: does it work for children with low socio-economic background?', *Advances in School Mental Health Promotion*, 2 (2): 51–60.

House of Commons Education and Skills Committee (2006) *Special Educational Needs: Third Report of the Session 2005–6*. London: HOCESC.

Hummel, S., Naylor, P., Chilcott, J., Guillaume, L., Wilkinson, A., Blank, L., Baxter, S. et al. (2009) *Cost-Effectiveness of Universal Interventions Which Aim to Promote Emotional and Social Wellbeing in Secondary Schools*. Sheffield: University of Sheffield.

Humphrey, N. (2009) 'SEAL: insufficient evidence?', *School Leadership Today*, 1 (3): 69–72.

Humphrey, N. (2012) 'The importance of evidence', *Behaviour and Pastoral Update*, 84 (February): 5.

Humphrey, N. and Ainscow, M. (2006) 'Transition club: facilitating learning, participation and psychological adjustment during the transition to secondary school', *European Journal of Psychology of Education*, 21 (3): 319–31.

Humphrey, N., Lendrum, A. and Wigelsworth, M. (2010) *Secondary Social and Emotional Aspects of Learning (SEAL): National Evaluation.* Nottingham: DFE Publications.

Humphrey, N., Lendrum, A., Wigelsworth, M. and Kalambouka, A. (2009) 'Primary SEAL group interventions: a qualitative study of factors affecting implementation and the role of Local Authority support', *International Journal of Emotional Education,* 1 (2): 34–54.

Humphrey, N., Curran, A., Morris, E., Farrell, P. and Woods, K. (2007) 'Emotional intelligence and education: a critical review', *Educational Psychology,* 27 (2): 235–54.

Humphrey, N., Kalambouka, A., Bolton, J., Lendrum, A., Wigelsworth, M., Lennie, C. and Farrell, P. (2008) *Primary Social and Emotional Aspects of Learning: Evaluation of Small Group Work.* Nottingham: DCSF Publications.

Humphrey, N., Kalambouka, A., Wigelsworth, M., Lendrum, A., Deighton, J. and Wolpert, M. (2011) 'Measures of social and emotional skills for children and young people: a systematic review', *Educational and Psychological Measurement,* 71 (4): 617–37.

Immordino-Yang, M. H. and Damasio, A. (2007) 'We feel, therefore we learn: the relevance of affective and social neuroscience to education', *Mind, Brain, and Education,* 1 (1): 3–10.

Institute for Public Policy Research (2006) *Freedom's Orphans: Raising Youth in a Changing World.* London: IPPR.

Institute of Education Sciences (2007) *What Works Clearinghouse: Caring School Community.* Washington, DC: IES.

Institute of Government and Public Affairs (2011) *Social and Emotional Learning for Illinois Students: Policy, Practice and Progress.* Chicago: IGPA.

Jacobson, N. S. and Follette, W. C. (1984) 'Psychotherapy outcome research: methods for reporting variability and evaluating clinical significance', *Behavior Therapy,* 15 (4): 336–52.

Jacobson, N. S. and Truax, P. (1991) 'Clinical significance: a statistical approach to determining meaningful change in psychotherapy research', *Journal of Consulting and Clinical Psychology,* 59 (1): 12–19.

Jennings, P. A. and Greenberg, M. T. (2009) 'The prosocial classroom: teacher social and emotional competence in relation to student and classroom outcomes', *Review of Educational Research,* 79 (1): 491–525.

Johnston, C. and Gowers, S. (2005) 'Routine outcome measurement: a survey of UK Child and Adolescent Mental Health Services', *Child and Adolescent Mental Health,* 10 (3): 133–9.

Jones, S. M., Brown, J. L., Hoglund, W. L. G. and Aber, J. L. (2010) 'A school-randomized clinical trial of an integrated social-emotional learning and literacy intervention: impacts after 1 school year', *Journal of Consulting and Clinical Psychology,* 78 (6): 829–42.

Joyce, B. and Showers, B. (2002) *Student Achievement Through Staff Development,* 3rd edn. Alexandria, VA: Association for Supervision and Curriculum Development.

Kam, C.-M., Greenberg, M. T. and Kusche, C. A. (2004) 'Sustained effects of the PATHS curriculum on the social and psychological adjustment of children in special education', *Journal of Emotional and Behavioral Disorders,* 12 (2): 66–78.

Kam, C.-M., Greenberg, M. T. and Walls, C. T. (2003) 'Examining the role of implementation quality in school-based prevention using the PATHS curriculum', *Prevention Science*, 4 (1): 55–63.

Kimber, B. (2011a) 'Social and emotional training in school: a contentious matter in Sweden', in J. O'Dea (ed.), *Current Issues and Controversies in School and Community Health, Sport and Physical Education*. Hauppage, NY: NOVA Publishers.

Kimber, B. (2011b) *Primary Prevention of Mental Health Problems Among Children and Adolescents Through Social and Emotional Training in School*. Stockholm: Karolinska Institutet.

Kimber, B., Sandell, R. and Bremberg, S. (2008) 'Social and emotional training in Swedish classrooms for the promotion of mental health: results from an effectiveness study in Sweden', *Health Promotion International*, 23 (2): 134–43.

Klein, J. B., Jacobs, R. H. and Reinecke, M. A. (2007) 'Cognitive-behavioral therapy for adolescent depression: a meta-analytic investigation of changes in effect-size estimates', *Journal of the American Academy of Child and Adolescent Psychiatry*, 46 (11): 1403–13.

Knoff, H. and Prout, H. (1985) *The Kinetic Drawing System: Family and School*. Los Angeles: Western Psychological Services.

Kohn, A. (1997) 'How not to teach values: a critical look at character education', *Phi Delta Kappan*, 78 (6): 428–39.

Kom, D. (2011) 'Social and emotional education in Singapore', in Marcelino Botín Foundation (ed.), *Social and Emotional Education: An International Analysis*. Santander, Spain: MBF, p. 45.

Kress, J. S., Norris, J. A., Schoenholz, D. A., Elias, M. J. and Seigle, P. (2004) 'Bringing together educational standards and social and emotional learning: making the case for educators', *American Journal of Education*, 111 (1): 68–89.

Kuperminc, G. P., Leadbeater, B. J. and Blatt, S. J. (2001) 'School social climate and individual differences in vulnerability to psychopathology among middle school students', *Journal of School Psychology*, 39 (2): 141–59.

Leithwood, K., Harris, A. and Hopkins, D. (2008) 'Seven strong claims about successful school leadership', *School Leadership and Management*, 28 (1): 27–42.

Lendrum, A. (2010) *Implementing Social and Emotional Aspects of Learning (SEAL) in Secondary Schools in England: Issues and Implications*. Manchester: University of Manchester.

Lendrum, A. and Humphrey, N. (2012) 'The importance of studying the implementation of school-based interventions', *Oxford Review of Education*, 38 (5): 635–52.

Lendrum, A., Humphrey, N. and Wigelsworth, M. (2012) 'Social and emotional aspects of learning (SEAL) for secondary schools: implementation difficulties and their implications for school-based mental health promotion', *Child and Adolescent Mental Health*.

Lerner, R. M. (1995) *America's Youth in Crisis: Challenges and Options for Programs and Policies*. Thousand Oaks, CA: Sage.

Lewis, M., Schaps, E. and Watson, M. (2003) 'The Child Development Project', in M. Elias, H. Arnold and C. Stegier Hussey (eds), *EQ+IQ: How to Build Smart, Nonviolent, Emotionally Intelligent Schools*. Thousand Oaks, CA: Corwin Press, pp. 100–8.

Little, M. and Hopkins, C. (2010) 'Will PATHS lead to the 4th "R"?', *Better: Evidence-based Education*, 2: 8–9.

Locke, E. A. (2005) 'Why emotional intelligence is an invalid concept', *Journal of Organizational Behavior*, 26 (4): 425–31.

McCabe, C. (2008) *Estimating the Short-Term Cost-Effectiveness of a Mental Health Promotion Intervention in Primary Schools*. Leeds: University of Leeds.

McConaughy, S. and Achenbach, T. (2001) *Manual for the Semi-Structured Clinical Interview for Children and Adolescents*. Burlington, VT: Research Center for Children, Youth and Families.

McGilloway, S., Hyland, L., Mháille, G., Lodge, A., Neill, D., Kelly, P., Leckey, Y., Bywater, T., Comiskey, C. and Donnelly, M. (2010) *Positive Classrooms, Positive Children: A Randomised Controlled Trial to Investigate the Effectiveness of the Incredible Years Teacher Classroom Management Programme in an Irish Context*. Belfast: Archways.

Mclaughlin, J. and Jordan, G. (1999) 'Logic models: a tool for telling your program's performance story', *Evaluation and Program Planning*, 22 (1): 65–72.

McLaughlin, K. A. (2011) 'The public health impact of major depression: a call for interdisciplinary prevention efforts', *Prevention Science*, 12 (4): 361–71.

McMahon, S., Washburn, J., Felix, E. and Yakin, J. (2000) 'Violence prevention: program effects on urban preschool and kindergarten children', *Applied and Preventive Psychology*, 9: 271–81.

Malti, T., Ribeaud, D. and Eisner, M. P. (2011) 'The effectiveness of two universal preventive interventions in reducing children's externalizing behavior: a cluster randomized controlled trial', *Journal of Clinical Child and Adolescent Psychology*, 40 (5): 677–92.

Marcelino Botín Foundation (2011) *Social and Emotional Education: An International Analysis*. Santander, Spain: Marcelino Botín Foundation.

Masten, A. S. and Obradovic, J. (2006) 'Competence and resilience in development', *Annals of the New York Academy of Sciences*, 1094: 13–27.

Matson, J. L., Rotatori, A. F. and Helsel, W. J. (1983) 'Development of a rating scale to measure social skills in children: the Matson Evaluation of Social Skills with Youngsters (MESSY)', *Behaviour Research and Therapy*, 21 (4): 335–40.

Matthews, G., Roberts, R. D. and Zeidner, M. (2004) 'Seven myths about emotional intelligence', *Psychological Inquiry*, 15 (3): 179–96.

Mavroveli, S., Petrides, K. V., Sangareau, Y. and Furnham, A. (2009) 'Exploring the relationships between trait emotional intelligence and objective socio-emotional outcomes in childhood', *British Journal of Educational Psychology*, 79 (2): 259–72.

Mayer, J. D. and Cobb, C. D. (2000) 'Educational policy on emotional intelligence: does it make sense?', *Educational Psychology Review*, 12 (2): 21.

Mayer, J. D., Roberts, R. D. and Barsade, S. G. (2008) 'Human abilities: emotional intelligence', *Annual Review of Psychology*, 59: 507–36.

Mayer, J. D., Salovey, P. and Caruso, D. R. (2008) 'Emotional intelligence: new ability or eclectic traits?', *American Psychologist*, 63 (6): 503–17.

Mayer, J. D., Salovey, P. and Caruso, D. R. (n.d.) *Mayer-Salovey-Caruso Emotional Intelligence Test: Youth Version – Research Edition*. Toronto: MHS.

Melde, C., Esbensen, F.-A. and Tusinski, K. (2006) 'Addressing program fidelity using onsite observations and program provider descriptions of program delivery', *Evaluation Review*, 30 (6): 714–40.

Merrell, K. W. (2008) *Behavioural, Social, and Emotional Assessment of Children and Adolescents*, 3rd edn. Oxford: Routledge.

Merrell, K. W. and Gueldner, B. A. (2010) *Social and Emotional Learning in the Classroom: Promoting Mental Health and Academic Success*. London: Guilford Press.

Merrell, K. W., Felver-Gant, J. C. and Tom, K. M. (2010) 'Development and validation of a parent report measure for assessing social-emotional competencies of children and adolescents', *Journal of Child and Family Studies*, 20 (4): 529–40.

Milne, J. (2008) 'Teachers' wasted study on popular emotional literacy course', *Times Education Supplement*, 10 October.

Ministry of Education (2001) *Desired Outcomes of Education*. Singapore: MIE.

Muldoon, O. (2004) 'Children of the Troubles: the impact of political violence in Northern Ireland', *Journal of Social Issues*, 60: 453–68.

National Agency for Education (2006) *Curriculum Plan for Public Schools, Preschool Classes and Leisure Centres*. Stockholm: NAE.

National Research Council and Institute of Medicine (2009) *Preventing Mental, Emotional and Behavioral Disorders Among Young People: Progress and Possibilities*. Washington, DC: NRCIM.

NICE (2008) *Promoting Children's Social and Emotional Wellbeing in Primary Education*. London: NICE.

Northen, S. (2012) 'Schools strive for pupils' happiness', *The Guardian*, 16 October.

O'Connell, M., Boat, T. and Warner, K. E. (2009) *Preventing Mental, Emotional, and Behavioral Disorders Among Young People: Progress and Possibilities*. Washington, DC: National Academies Press.

O'Reilly, D. and Stevenson, M. (2003) 'Mental health in Northern Ireland: have the Troubles made it worse?', *Journal of Epidemiology and Community Health*, 57: 488–92.

Park, J. (2011) 'The importance of school ethos', *Antidote Blog*. Retrieved from http://www.antidote.org.uk/the-importance-of-school-ethos/.

Parker, J. D. A., Creque, R. E., Barnhart, D. L., Harris, J. I., Majeski, S. A., Wood, L. M., Bond, B. J. et al. (2004) 'Academic achievement in high school: does emotional intelligence matter?', *Personality and Individual Differences*, 37 (7): 1321–30.

Partnership Management Board (2007) *Personal Development and Mutual Understanding for Key Stages 1 and 2*. Belfast: CCEA.

Paul, R. and Elder, L. (2007) *A Critical Thinker's Guide to Educational Fads*. Tomales, CA: Critical Thinking Press.

Pellegrini, A. D. and Bartini, M. (2000) 'A longitudinal study of bullying, victimisation and peer affiliation during the transition from primary to middle school', *American Educational Research Journal*, 37 (3): 699–725.

Pellegrini, A. D. and Long, J. D. (2002) 'A longitudinal study of bullying, dominance, and victimization during the transition from primary school through secondary school', *British Journal of Developmental Psychology*, 20 (2): 259–80.

Penza, S., Zeman, J. and Shipman, K. (1998). *Validation of the Emotion Dysregulation Scale for Children (EDS)*. Poster presented at the Conference on Human Development, Mobile, AL.

Perlis, R. H., Perlis, C. S., Wu, Y., Hwang, C., Joseph, M. and Nierenberg, A. A. (2005) 'Industry sponsorship and financial conflict of interest in the reporting of clinical trials in psychiatry', *American Journal of Psychiatry*, 162 (10): 1957–60.

Peters, C., Kranzler, J. H. and Rossen, E. (2009) 'Validity of the Mayer-Salovey-Caruso Emotional Intelligence Test: Youth Version – Research Edition', *Canadian Journal of School Psychology*, 24 (1): 76–81.

Petrides, K. V. and Furnham, A. (2001) 'Trait emotional intelligence: psychometric investigation with reference to established trait taxonomies', *European Journal of Personality*, 15 (6): 425–48.

Petrides, K. V., Frederickson, N. and Furnham, A. (2004) 'The role of trait emotional intelligence in academic performance and deviant behavior at school', *Personality and Individual Differences*, 36 (2): 277–93.

Petrides, K. V., Sangareau, Y., Furnham, A. and Frederickson, N. (2006) 'Trait emotional intelligence and children's peer relations at school', *Social Development*, 15 (3): 537–47.

Petrosino, A. and Soydan, H. (2005) 'The impact of program developers as evaluators on criminal recidivism: results from meta-analyses of experimental and quasi-experimental research', *Journal of Experimental Criminology*, 1 (4): 435–50.

Posse, M., Hällström, T. and Backenroth-Ohsako, G. (2002) 'Alexithymia, social support, psycho-social stress and mental health in a female population', *Nordic Journal of Psychiatry*, 56 (5): 329–34.

Poulou, M. (2007) 'Social resilience within a social and emotional learning framework: the perceptions of teachers in Greece', *Emotional and Behavioural Difficulties*, 12 (2): 91–104.

Rae-Grant, N., Thomas, B. H., Offord, D. R. and Boyle, M. H. (1989) 'Risk, protective factors, and the prevalence of behavioral and emotional disorders in children and adolescents', *Journal of the American Academy of Child and Adolescent Psychiatry*, 28 (2): 262–8.

Ransford, C., Greenberg, M., Domitrovich, C. E., Small, M. and Jacobson, L. (2009) 'The role of teachers' psychological experiences and perceptions of curriculum supports on the implementation of a social and emotional learning curriculum', *School Psychology Review*, 38 (4): 510–32.

Raudenbush, S. (2008) 'Advancing educational policy by advancing research on instruction', *American Educational Research Journal*, 45 (1): 206–30.

Reicher, H. (2010) 'Building inclusive education on social and emotional learning: challenges and perspectives – a review', *International Journal of Inclusive Education*, 14 (3): 213–46.

Resnicow, K., Davis, M., Smith, M., Lazarus-Yaroch, A., Baranowski, T., Baranowski, J., Doyle, C. et al. (1998) 'How best to measure implementation of school health curricula: a comparison of three measures', *Health Education Research*, 13 (2): 239–50.

Reyes, M. R., Brackett, M. A., Rivers, S. E., Elbertson, N. A. and Salovey, P. (2012) 'The interaction effects of program training, dosage, and implementation quality on targeted student outcomes for the RULER approach to social and emotional learning', *School Psychology Review*, 41 (1): 82–99.

Riggs, N. R., Greenberg, M. T., Kusché, C. A. and Pentz, M. A. (2006) 'The mediational role of neurocognition in the behavioral outcomes of a social-emotional prevention program in elementary school students: effects of the PATHS Curriculum', *Prevention Science*, 7 (1): 91–102.

Rimm-Kaufman, S. E., Fan, X., Chiu, Y.-J. and You, W. (2007) 'The contribution of the Responsive Classroom approach on children's academic achievement: results from a three-year longitudinal study', *Journal of School Psychology*, 45 (4): 401–21.

Romano, E., Babchishin, L., Pagani, L. S. and Kohen, D. (2010) 'School readiness and later achievement: replication and extension using a nationwide Canadian survey', *Developmental Psychology*, 46 (5): 995–1007.

Rosenblatt, J. L. and Elias, M. J. (2008) 'Dosage effects of a preventive social-emotional learning intervention on achievement loss associated with middle school transition', *Journal of Primary Prevention*, 29 (6): 535–55.

Saarni, C. (1999) *The Development of Emotional Competence*. New York: Guilford Press.

Salovey, P. and Mayer, J. (1990) 'Emotional intelligence', *Imagination, Cognition and Personality*, 9 (2): 185–211.

Sánchez, V., Steckler, A., Nitirat, P., Hallfors, D., Cho, H. and Brodish, P. (2007) 'Fidelity of implementation in a treatment effectiveness trial of Reconnecting Youth', *Health Education Research*, 22 (1): 95–107.

Sanders, M., Turner, K. and Markie-Dadds, C. (2002) 'The development and dissemination of the Triple P Positive Parenting Program: a multi-level, evidence-based system of parenting and family support', *Prevention Science*, 3 (3): 173–89.

Schultz, D., Izard, C. E. and Bear, G. (2004) 'Children's emotion processing: relations to emotionality and aggression', *Development and psychopathology*, 16 (2): 371–87.

Schweinhart, L. J., Montie, J., Xiang, Z., Barnett, W. S., Belfield, C. R. and Nores, M. (2005) *The High Scope Perry Preschool Study Through Age 40: Summary, Conclusions and Frequently Asked Questions*. Ypsilanti, MI: High Scope Press.

Sharp, P. (2000) 'Promoting emotional literacy: emotional literacy improves and increases your life chances', *Pastoral Care in Education*, 18 (3): 8–10.

Sheffield, J. K., Spence, S. H., Rapee, R. M., Kowalenko, N. K., Wignall, A., Davis, A. and McLoone, J. (2006) 'Evaluation of universal, indicated and combined cognitive-behavioural approaches to the prevention of depression among adolescents', *Journal of Consulting and Clinical Psychology*, 74 (1): 66–79.

Shuayb, M. and O'Donnell, S. (2008) *Aims and Values in Primary Education: England and Other Countries*. Cambridge: Cambridge University Press.

Shucksmith, J. (2007) *Mental Wellbeing of Children in Primary Education (Targeted/Indicated Activities)*. Teeside: University of Teeside.

Shucksmith, J., Spratt, J., Philip, K. and McNaughton, R. (2009) *A Critical Review of the Literature on Children and Young People's Views of the Factors That Influence Their Mental Health*. Edinburgh: NHS Scotland.

Slee, P., Lawson, M., Russell, A., Askell-Williams, H., Dix, K., Owens, L., Skrzypiec, G. et al. (2009) *KidsMatter Primary Evaluation Final Report*. Flinders, South Australia: Flinders University.

Smith, J., Schneider, B. and Smith, P. (2004) 'The effectiveness of whole-school antibullying programs: a synthesis of evaluation research', *School Psychology Review*, 33 (4): 547–60.

Social and Character Development Research Consortium (2010) *Efficacy of School-Wide Programs to Promote Social and Character Development and Reduce Problem Behavior in Elementary School Children*. Washington, DC: SACDRC.

Solomon, D., Battistich, V., Watson, M., Schaps, E. and Lewis, C. (2000) 'A six-district study of educational change: direct and mediated effects of the Child Development Project', *Social Psychology of Education*, 4 (1): 3–51.

Southampton Psychology Service (2003) *Emotional Literacy: Assessment and Intervention*. London: Nfer Nelson.

Stallard, P., Simpson, N., Anderson, S., Carter, T., Osborn, C. and Bush, S. (2005) 'An evaluation of the FRIENDS programme: a cognitive behaviour therapy intervention to promote emotional resilience', *Archives of Disease in Childhood*, 90 (10): 1016–9.

Statham, J. and Chase, E. (2010) *Childhood Wellbeing: A Brief Overview*. London: Institute of Education.

Sternberg, R. (2002) 'Foreword', in G. Matthews and M. Zeidner (eds), *Emotional Intelligence: Science and Myth*. Boston: MIT Press, pp. xi–xv.

Stewart, E. B. (2007) 'School structural characteristics, student effort, peer associations, and parental involvement: the influence of school- and individual-level factors on academic achievement', *Education and Urban Society*, 40 (2): 179–204.

Terwee, C. B., Bot, S. D. M., de Boer, M. R., van der Windt, D. A. W. M., Knol, D. L., Dekker, J., Bouter, L. M. et al. (2007) 'Quality criteria were proposed for measurement properties of health status questionnaires', *Journal of Clinical Epidemiology*, 60 (1): 34–42.

Thorndike, R. L. and Stein, S. (1937) 'An evaluation of the attempts to measure social intelligence', *Psychological Bulletin*, 34: 275–85.

UNICEF (2007) *An Overview of Child Well-Being in Rich Countries*. Florence: UNICEF.

US Department of Health and Human Services (2010) *Health-Risk Behaviors and Academic Achievement*. Atlanta, GA: USDHHS.

Van Horn, M. L., Atkins-Burnett, S., Karlin, E., Ramey, S. L. and Snyder, S. (2007) 'Parent ratings of children's social skills: longitudinal psychometric analyses of the Social Skills Rating System', *School Psychology Quarterly*, 22 (2): 162–99.

Vostanis, P., Humphrey, N., Fitzgerald, N., Wolpert, M. and Deighton, J. (2012) 'How do schools promote emotional wellbeing among their pupils? Findings from a national scoping survey of mental health provision in English schools', *Child and Adolescent Mental Health*, iFirst.

Waterhouse, L. (2006) 'Multiple intelligences, the Mozart effect, and emotional intelligence: a critical review', *Educational Psychologist*, 41 (4): 207–25.

Watson, D., Emery, C. and Bayliss, P. (2012) *Children's Social and Emotional Wellbeing in Schools: A Critical Perspective*. Bristol: Policy Press.

Weare, K. (2004) *Developing the Emotionally Literate School*. London: Sage.

Weare, K. (2010) 'Mental health and social and emotional learning: evidence, principles, tensions, balances', *Advances in School Mental Health Promotion*, 3 (1): 5–17.

Weare, K. and Gray, G. (2003) *What Works in Promoting Children's Emotional and Social Competence and Wellbeing?* Nottingham: DfES Publications.

Weare, K. and Markham, W. (2005) 'What do we know about promoting mental health through schools?', *Promotion and Education*, 12 (3): 4–8.

Weare, K. and Nind, M. (2011) *Promoting Mental Health of Children and Adolescents Through Schools and School-Based Interventions.* Southampton: University of Southampton.

Weisz, J. R., Sandler, I. N., Durlak, J. A. and Anton, B. S. (2005) 'Promoting and protecting youth mental health through evidence-based prevention and treatment', *American Psychologist*, 60 (6): 628–48.

Wells, J., Barlow, J. and Stewart-Brown, S. (2003) 'A systematic review of universal approaches to mental health promotion in schools', *Health Education*, 103 (4): 197–220.

Wigelsworth, M., Humphrey, N. and Lendrum, A. (2012) 'Evaluation of a school-wide preventive intervention for adolescents: the secondary social and emotional aspects of learning (SEAL) programme', *School Mental Health*, iFirst.

Wigelsworth, M., Humphrey, N., Kalambouka, A. and Lendrum, A. (2010) 'A review of key issues in the measurement of children's social and emotional skills', *Educational Psychology in Practice*, 26 (2): 173–86.

Willhelm, O. (2005) 'Measures of emotional intelligence: practice and standards', in R. Schulze and R. D. Roberts (eds), *Emotional Intelligence: An International Handbook*. Cambridge, MA: Hogrefe & Huber, pp. 131–54.

Wilson, S. J. and Lipsey, M. W. (2007) 'School-based interventions for aggressive and disruptive behavior: update of a meta-analysis', *American Journal of Preventive Medicine*, 33 (2 Suppl.): S130–43.

Wolpert, M. et al. (2008) *Review and Recommendations for National Policy for England for the Use of Mental Health Outcome Measures with Children and Young People*. Nottingham: DCSF Publications.

Wolpert, M. et al. (2011) *Me and My School: Findings from the National Evaluation of Targeted Mental Health in Schools*. Nottingham: DFE Publications.

Wyn, J., Cahill, H., Holdsworth, R., Rowling, L. and Carson, S. (2000) 'MindMatters, a whole-school approach promoting mental health and wellbeing', *Australasian Psychiatry*, 34 (4): 594–601.

Yeaton, W. H. and Sechrest, L. (1981) 'Critical dimensions in the choice and maintenance of successful treatments: strength, integrity, and effectiveness', *Journal of Consulting and Clinical Psychology*, 49 (2): 156–67.

Zeidner, M., Roberts, R. D. and Matthews, G. (2002) 'Can emotional intelligence be schooled? A critical review', *Educational Psychologist*, 37 (4): 215–31.

Zins, J. and Elias, M. J. (2007) 'Social and emotional learning: promoting the development of all students', *Journal of Educational and Psychological Consultation*, 17 (2–3): 233–55.

Zins, J. E., Bloodworth, M. R., Weissberg, R. P. and Walberg, H. J. (2004) 'The scientific base linking social and emotional learning to school success', in J. E. Zins, R. P. Weissberg, M. C. Wang and H. J. Walberg (eds), *Building Academic Success on Social and Emotional Learning: What Does the Research Say?* New York: Teachers College Press, pp. 3–22.

Index

Bold numbers denote main reference